Best Practices in Assessment of Symptom and Performance Validity

About the Author

Joseph L. Etherton, PhD, ABPP, is a professor in the Psychology Department at Texas State University, San Marcos, TX, USA. He completed his PhD in clinical psychology at the University of Georgia. He is a licensed psychologist and board-certified in clinical psychology. His research has addressed psychosocial factors influencing outcome following injury, including the effects of pain on cognitive functioning. He has taught undergraduate courses in psychopathology, psychometrics, and research design, and graduate courses in psychopathology and neuropsychological assessment.

Book Editors

Amitai Abramovitch, PhD, Adjunct Associate Professor, Department of Psychology, University of Texas at Austin, TX

Dean McKay, PhD, ABPP, Professor, Department of Psychology, Fordham University, NY

Best Practices in Assessment of Symptom and Performance Validity

Joseph L. Etherton
Department of Psychology, Texas State University,
San Marcos, TX

hogrefe

Library of Congress Cataloging in Publication information for the print version of this book is available via the Library of Congress Marc Database under the LC Control Number 2026935285

Library and Archives Canada Cataloguing in Publication
Title: Best practices in assessment of symptom and performance validity / Joseph L. Etherton, Department of Psychology, Texas State University, San Marcos, TX.
Names: Etherton, Joseph L., author.
Description: Includes bibliographical references.
Identifiers: Canadiana (print) 2026014049X | Canadiana (ebook) 20260154490 | ISBN 9780889376700 (softcover) | ISBN 9781616766702 (PDF) | ISBN 9781613346709 (EPUB)
Subjects: LCSH: Neuropsychological tests. | LCSH: Factitious disorders—Diagnosis. | LCSH: Malingering—Diagnosis.
Classification: LCC RC386.6.N48 E84 2026 | DDC 616.8/0475—dc23

www.hogrefe.com

PUBLISHING OFFICES
USA: Hogrefe Publishing Corporation, 44 Merrimac St., Newburyport, MA 01950
Phone 978 255 3700, E-mail customersupport@hogrefe.com
EUROPE: Hogrefe Publishing GmbH, Merkelstr. 3, 37085 Göttingen, Germany
Phone +49 551 99950 0, Fax +49 551 99950 111; E-mail publishing@hogrefe.com
SALES & DISTRIBUTION
USA: Hogrefe Publishing, Casemate Publishers & Book Distribution,
22835 Quicksilver Drive, Dulles, VA 20166
Phone 610 853 9131; E-mail customersupport@hogrefe.com
UK: Hogrefe Ltd, Hogrefe House, Albion Place, Oxford, OX1 1QZ
Phone +44 186 579 7920; E-Mail customersupport@hogrefe.co.uk
EUROPE: Hogrefe Publishing, Merkelstr. 3, 37085 Göttingen, Germany
Phone +49 551 99950 0, Fax +49 551 99950 111; E-mail publishing@hogrefe.com
OTHER OFFICES
CANADA: Hogrefe Publishing, 82 Laird Drive, East York, Ontario, M4G 3V1
SWITZERLAND: Hogrefe Publishing, Langgass-Strasse 76, 3012 Bern

Printed and bound in the USA

ISBN 978-0-88937-670-0 (print) • ISBN 978-1-61676-670-2 (PDF) • ISBN 978-1-61334-670-9 (EPUB)
https://doi.org/10.1027/00670-000

Dedication

To my dear wife Karen, and our wonderful sons Jack and Bobby.

And with gratitude to Kevin Bianchini and Kevin Greve, whose mentorship in research and clinical applications of validity assessment has been invaluable.

Contents

Chapter 1
Introduction

In the movie "E.T. The Extraterrestrial" (Spielberg, 1982) there is a scene in which Elliott, the young protagonist, urgently needs to stay home from school to take care of E.T., the alien creature he has just met. Because he does not yet want to tell his mother about E.T., he needs a compelling reason for missing school, and the classic reason for missing school is being sick. Although Elliott cannot simply make himself ill on demand, he can create the appearance of being sick, in part by lying in bed groaning and speaking in a weak voice and "acting" sick (which he does). But because his mother may not accept these signs as legitimate proof of illness, Elliott takes a thermometer, holds it under a lamp to raise the temperature on the thermometer, and then allows his mother to read the elevated temperature as proof that he has a fever. Elliott has taken a reliable instrument for measuring temperature and detecting fever (the thermometer) and distorted its output (the temperature reading) to mislead others about his actual status.

In psychological assessment, we use a variety of measures to gather information from people about their mood, their preferences, their personality traits, and their typical patterns of behavior. For example, a self-report measure of depression may include items asking how frequently or how intensely one experiences sleep disturbance, feelings of worthlessness, inability to enjoy activities, and other symptoms of depression. The examinee may attempt to be completely accurate and forthright in responding to the questions, in which case we would have a fairly accurate estimate of the person's depression severity. However, someone who wanted to feign depression so they can receive compensated time for work for a psychological disability, or so they can be discharged from unwanted military service, may untruthfully endorse items that create the appearance of severe depression, such that the resulting test scores would present a picture of the examinee that would be far from accurate.

The forensic psychologist Richard Rogers wrote that "nearly all psychological measures are based on three unballasted [i.e., lacking weight or support] assumptions: that each patient (1) is psychologically engaged in the assessment process, (2) shares the same goals as the clinician, and (3) cooperates with the clinician's methods of achieving these goals" (Rogers, 2001, p. 405). We cannot assume that the examinee is engaged in the assessment process because some examinees are unmotivated, indifferent, or even hostile to the assessment process. Examinees may not share the same goals as the clinician when the examinee very much wants a certain outcome (e.g., a particular diagnosis) while the clinician's goal may be to accurately characterize the examinee, whether the outcome is favorable to the examinee or not. And we cannot assume that the examinee will cooperate with the process of reaching an accurate characterization of the examinee, because the examinee may very much wish to appear more psychologically healthy than is the case, in seeking child custody; or may wish to appear more impaired than is the case, as when pursuing a disability claim.

Given that some examinees may be motivated to avoid helping the clinician develop an accurate understanding of their psychological status, it is important for clinicians to consider whether the examinee has misrepresented themselves, and to examine objective indicators of the validity of the examinee's self-reported statements and item responses.

Psychological assessment involves using a variety of different methods to gather information about a person. The types of information to be gathered depend on the purpose of the evaluation, but may include information about their personality traits, whether they have symptoms of a psychological disorder, their preferences, concerns, strengths, weaknesses, and so on.

Information from psychological assessments may be used to determine whether someone meets criteria for a psychological disorder, whether they are suitable for hire as a police officer, whether they have the capacity to make their own important decisions, among others. Importantly, information from psychological assessments depends in large part on whether the person is providing accurate information. To the extent that a person attempts to present themselves in a manner that is different from how they actually are, the results of psychological assessment will be inaccurate. For example, someone who wants others to conclude that they have a psychological disorder may report having symptoms or problems that they do not actually have or may exaggerate symptoms that they do have. In addition, test results may lead to an inaccurate perception of an examinee when the examinee responds somewhat randomly because of factors such as indifference to testing, inability to understand test items, or inattention to the items.

Validity assessment broadly speaking refers to a variety of different methods and measures used to evaluate whether the data obtained from an evaluation accurately characterizes the examinee in terms of psychological symptoms, cognitive abilities, or other relevant domains. Validity assessment tools may indicate whether an examinee appears to be feigning psychological problems or cognitive deficits, and whether they appear to have tried their best on cognitive tasks or given forthright responses to questions. Including validity measures in assessments helps to ensure that the results of testing can be trusted as legitimate and helps to identify cases in which the examiner should consider test results as invalid. The purpose of this book is to describe methods that clinicians use to evaluate the validity of an examinee's presentation during assessment and the rationale for their use, review research findings regarding the accuracy of various methods in detecting invalid examinee presentations and describe how to integrate validity assessment methods in a typical psychological or neuropsychological evaluation.

The current chapter will introduce some of the conceptual background and terminology used in validity assessment, first by describing incentives for disability exaggeration and the contexts in which invalid responding related to disability exaggeration typically occurs. This chapter will also introduce some of the different methods used to assess the validity of an examinee's presentation during assessment, and terms related to different forms of invalidity.

Assessing Validity Related to Disability Exaggeration

Disability Incentives

There are a number of different situations that involve incentives to appear impaired or affected by some psychological condition or neurocognitive deficits. The incentives may be financial such as personal injury awards for a motor vehicle accident, a financial settlement for a workers compensation injury, or, disability benefits from a Social Security (or similar agency, depending on the country) disability case. Other forms of incentive include obtaining access to prescription medications by feigning or exaggerating pain. This book will focus primarily on cases involving claims of impairment due to a cognitive, physical, or psychological condition that the claimant attributes to an individual or company against whom they have filed some form of claim.

Primary, Secondary, and Tertiary Gain

The term "secondary gain" is sometimes used to refer to the financial incentive that plaintiffs seek. Originating in psychoanalysis, secondary gain refers to desirable consequences of developing symptoms above and beyond the "primary gain" that psychoanalysts describe as relief from an unconscious conflict experienced through symptom development (Fishbain et al., 1995). In addition to financial incentives, secondary gain may include receiving attention and sympathy from others as well as avoidance of undesirable obligations such as household tasks.

Related to the term secondary gain, tertiary gain refers to motivations that are experienced by individuals other than the patient (Kwan et al., 2001), such as attorneys and treating clinicians, who may benefit financially in proportion to the duration or severity of the patient's condition. The more severely impaired the patient, the greater the potential financial outcome is for an attorney representing them, as the attorney typically receives a percentage of the patient's settlement. Similarly, clinicians can continue to bill for treatment so long as the patient continues to experience symptoms.

Just as secondary gain has the potential to influence patient outcomes, tertiary gain may influence attorney or clinician actions in a way that tends to accentuate symptoms and problems, with the potential to delay recovery and return to normal life.

Clinical Pearl

In reviewing patient records keep in mind the potential influence of tertiary gain on treating clinicians.

Personal Injury Claims

Personal injury claims may be filed when someone alleges that they experienced physical or psychological harm from the actions or negligence of another individual or company. The plaintiff (the person making the claim) may seek compensation for lost wages, medical expenses, and future care. Personal injury settlements in the US vary significantly, with potential awards in the millions of dollars (e.g., Bayen et al., 2019). It has been estimated that disability exaggeration occurs in approximately 30–40% of personal injury cases, although these estimates vary by venue and by assessment methods (Larrabee, 2003b; Mittenberg et al., 2002).

Social Security Disability Claims

Social Security Disability Insurance (SSDI) and Supplemental Security Income (SSI) programs are intended to provide financial support for those with disabilities that prevent them from maintaining gainful employment.

Although the process for obtaining these benefits is nonadversarial in theory, in practice only around 30 % of applications are approved (Social Security Administration, 2021). The benefits from successful SSDI/SSI applications include modest monthly payments, as well as eligibility for Medicare and possible retroactive benefit payments. Although the initial financial gain for SSDI/SSI is relatively modest in comparison, with potentially large settlements from personal injury litigation, the cumulative benefits over years may be substantial. It has been estimated that disability exaggeration occurs in some 45 % to nearly 59 % of SSDI/SSI claims (Chafetz & Underhill, 2013; Larrabee, 2007).

Worker's Compensation Claims

Worker's Compensation systems in the US are typically state-administered programs intended to provide wage replacement benefits and medical care for work-related injuries while also protecting employers from most lawsuits related to the injury (most countries have similar programs). Injured workers typically receive a percentage of their regular salary while they are unable to work at their normal capacity. Injured workers may also receive a permanent disability settlement related to the severity of the injury. Worker's compensation cases may become adversarial if there is disagreement between the worker and employer or carrier about the nature and severity of the injury. It has been estimated that approximately 25–40 % of contested worker's compensation claims involve disability exaggeration (Greve, Ord et al., 2009).

Validity Assessment Methods

It is also important to distinguish between two different ways in which examinees can attempt to appear disabled. Suppose a man was claiming concussion-related disability in a personal injury lawsuit from a motor vehicle accident, even though he was not actually injured. The man could feign disability by endorsing various symptoms and deficits on a self-report measure that he does not actually experience, but that he believes will make him appear disabled. This involves symptom overreporting or symptom exaggeration. *Symptom Validity Measures* (or *Symptom Validity Tests*, often abbreviated as SVTs) are methods used in self-report tests to detect patterns of responding associated with exaggeration or fabrication of symptoms or deficits, or that otherwise reflect an attempt to appear impaired or disabled.

The man in this example may also feign disability by underperforming on neuropsychological assessment measures that assess cognitive ability, such as giving incorrect answers or working very slowly on a neuropsychological assessment for which timing influences the score. *Performance Validity Tests* (PVTs) are used to detect inadequate effort during testing, which may reflect lack of motivation or intentional underperformance. PVTs detect invalid *performance* rather than invalid *symptom reporting*, which may be detected by SVTs.

Notice that I wrote "may" be detected: neither SVTs nor PVTs are capable of detecting every instance of disability exaggeration. This is in part because different people have different ideas about what it means to appear disabled, and so some may not feign disability in ways that would be detected by some validity measures. In addition, most validity measures have some overlap in the range of scores produced by feigning patients and by legitimate (non-feigning) patients. This means that cutoff scores that will be used to detect feigning will need to be set in such a way as to avoid inaccurately classifying a legitimate examinee as feigning, such that some feigning examinees will remain undetected by that validity test. These issues relate to the *classification accuracy* of validity tests, a topic that will be covered in more detail in Chapter 2. The important point to remember for now is that no validity test performs perfectly in distinguishing feigning examinees from legitimate examinees, and so clinicians should not rely on the results of any single validity measure as a way of determining whether an examinee is or is not feigning.

It should be noted that earlier publications on validity assessment used the term "SVTs" to refer to what we would currently call performance validity measures; this was subsequently clarified by Larrabee (2012b), who recommended using the terms "*performance validity* to refer to the validity of actual ability task performance ... and *symptom validity* to refer to the accuracy of symptom complaint on self-report measures ..." (Larrabee, 2012b, p. 626). Although older papers on validity assessment may have used the term SVT to refer to measures of performance validity, this book will use the terms SVTs and PVTs to refer to measures of the validity of self-reported symptoms and the validity of task performance, respectively.

Assessing Self-Report Validity

On self-report assessment measures, an examinee's presentation can be invalid because of excessive inconsistencies in their responses to items, because they endorse symptoms or problems that they do not actually experience (overreporting), or because they deny common flaws or shortcomings that most people admit (underreporting). Both overreporting and underreporting are considered to reflect more intentional misrepresentation by the examinee, whereas inconsistent responding is generally regarded as reflecting inattention, difficulty understanding the items, or unwillingness to cooperate in the assessment, rather than intentional misrepresentation. Chapter 3 will review specific self-report measures in more detail. For now, we will introduce some of the most common types of self-report validity scales.

Validity Scales Within Psychological Measures

The three most commonly used broadband psychological measures all include validity scales that are produced as part of scoring along with their clinical scales. These include the Minnesota Multiphasic Personality Inventory (MMPI), different versions of which will be referenced in the book (MMPI-2; Butcher et al., 1989; MMPI-2-RF; Ben-Porath & Tellegen, 2008; and MMPI-3; Ben-Porath & Tellegen, 2020). For simplicity, the term MMPI will be used unless one of the versions is excluded. Also included are the Personality Assessment Inventory (PAI; Morey, 2007), and the Millon Clinical Multiaxial Inventory (MCMI-IV; Millon et al., 2015). Although earlier versions of the PAI and MCMI exist, only the most recent version will be reviewed in the book.

Each of these instruments has been in use for decades in clinical practice and research. Although the primary purpose of these instruments is to obtain psychological data about the examinee, each of the instruments has incorporated validity scales in order to detect patterns of invalid responding. There are three main types of invalid responding: overreporting, underreporting, and inconsistent responding.

Overreporting (Faking Bad)

Overreporting involves claiming or endorsing symptoms or problems to a greater degree of frequency or severity than is the case. The kinds of symptoms or problems that may be endorsed by an individual depends somewhat on what type of disability or condition they are trying to feign, and their perception of the kinds of symptoms or problems someone with the condition would experience. The validity scales that were developed for the MMPI, PAI, MCMI, and other forms of self-report validity scales rely in part on the disparity between the number and kinds of symptoms that patients with conditions such as schizophrenia, depression, or posttraumatic stress disorder (PTSD) actually experience, and the assumptions that people without these conditions have about the symptoms. The result is that people trying to feign a psychological condition or neuropsychological deficit will tend to report symptoms or impairment that actual patients endorse rarely or to a lesser extent; the more these kinds of responses occur, the more elevated the validity scales become.

It should be noted that symptom overreporting may reflect differing degrees of conscious awareness and differing degrees of intensity. For example, although some examinees consciously and intentionally respond inaccurately to try to appear disabled, in the case of *somatization*, the individual has little or no conscious awareness that they are overreporting symptoms. Such individuals tend to experience subjective physical symptoms in response to stress but lack awareness of this process. Consequently, they may report or endorse excessive physical/medical symptoms as an expression of their distress, but without the awareness or intent to deceive.

Underreporting (Faking Good)

In some assessment situations the examinee will be motivated to appear more psychologically healthy or more virtuous than is the case. The MMPI, PAI, and MCMI all include scales to detect when someone has responded in a way that presents the examinee in an unrealistically favorable light. Underreporting validity scales are more likely to be elevated in situations involving an incentive to appear psychologically healthy, such as child custody evaluations or pre-employment psychological testing for first-responder applicants. However, in the context of disability-related assessments, some individuals will respond in a way that emphasizes their virtue as part of an overall strategy of emphasizing a lack of flaws or problems except for those ostensibly caused by the injury. As a result, such examinees may have elevations on some overreporting validity scales while also having an elevated underreporting type of validity scale. In the case of the MMPI, this could be reflected in an elevated score on the underreporting L scale ("Uncommon virtues") along with an elevated overreporting Response Bias Scale (RBS), which reflects an unusual combination of responses associated with noncredible memory complaints. Interpretive guidelines caution that modest MMPI L scale elevations may occur in honest responders from a background that stresses traditional values (Ben-Porath & Tellegen, 2020)

The PAI has an underreporting validity scale called Positive Impression (PIM) that, at sufficiently elevated levels, suggests that the PAI clinical scales are likely questionable because the degree of denial of ordinary shortcomings likely involves significant misrepresentation of one's psychological status. The Desirability Scale is the corresponding underreporting scale of the MCMI.

Noncontent ("Random") Responding

An examinee may be asked to complete a standardized self-report measure, but for a variety of reasons their responses may be unrelated to the content of the item. This can occur if the examinee is uncooperative, lacks motivation to participate, or is indifferent about the assessment such that they may respond randomly to items or may follow a pattern such as alternating between True and False, or giving all True or all False responses. This response style would result in test scores that would be invalid, because they would not bear any relationship to the examinee's actual psychological status. Noncontent responding may be detected by validity scales based on responses to items with related content that convey different meanings.

Stand-Alone Symptom Validity Measures

In addition to the validity scales included within clinical self-report measures such as the MMPI, PAI, and MCMI, a limited number of separate symptom validity measures have been developed. These measures are intended specifically to evaluate the validity of self-reported symptoms, deficits or problems. These include a self-report questionnaire, the Structured Inventory of Malingered Symptomatology (SIMS; Widows & Smith, 2005), as well as structured interviews administered verbally by the examiner: the Structured Interview of Reported Symptoms (SIRS; Rogers et al., 1992), and the Miller Forensic Assessment of Symptoms Test (M-FAST; Miller, 2001). These measures will be described in greater detail in Chapter 3.

Assessing Performance Validity

Validity measures that detect invalid performance, such as when an examinee intentionally provides incorrect responses on a memory task in order to seem impaired, are called Performance Validity Tests (PVTs). A rationale underlying many of these PVTs is that individuals attempting to appear disabled will not readily be able to calibrate how difficult different kinds of tasks are; if they are trying to perform in a way that makes them appear disabled, they will have to perform below their actual capabilities and so will have to make errors that they would not make naturally. PVTs take advantage of the fact that genuinely impaired individuals often have intact performance on certain types of tasks, whereas examinees attempting to feign impairment often perform poorly on such tasks.

Measures of performance validity may be derived from performance on an actual cognitive/neuropsychological task; these are called *embedded* PVTs. Examples of embedded PVTs include Reliable Digit Span, which can be derived from patterns of scores on the Wechsler-based Digit Span task. Other measures of performance validity are separate, "stand alone" tasks that are administered in addition to the neuropsychological or cognitive tasks in an assessment. These include the Test of Memory Malingering (TOMM; Tombaugh, 1996) and the Word Memory Test (WMT; Green, 2003); these and other performance validity measures will be reviewed in more detail in Chapter 3.

Malingering

Malingering involves the intentional production or exaggeration of symptoms or deficits in pursuit of some external incentive. Situations in which malingering may occur include personal injury litigation, worker's compensation, and Social Security disability claims, all of which involve financial incentives to appear impaired. Malingering may also occur in situations in which being perceived as impaired or disabled may allow the individual to avoid military service, or to avoid or reduce the severity of criminal penalties.

Diagnostic frameworks have been developed for diagnosing malingered neurocognitive dysfunction (Slick et al., 1999), as well as malingered pain-related disability (Bianchini et al., 2005). These diagnostic frameworks highlight the fact that individuals can emphasize impairment in different functional domains; for example, someone involved in personal injury litigation following a motor vehicle accident may exaggerate primarily cognitive deficits, such as attention or memory problems, whereas another person may emphasize primarily physical impairment that they attribute to pain. These diagnostic frameworks incorporate information from both SVTs (Symptom Validity Tests) and PVTs (Performance Validity Tests) and provide a systematic method for drawing inferences about the likelihood that an individual is malingering. These diagnostic frameworks will be described in more detail in Chapter 2, which describes methods for identifying malingering of neurocognitive dysfunction (Slick et al., 1999) and for identifying malingering related to pain complaints (Bianchini et al., 2005). In addition, Chapter 2 will review theoretical underpinnings and concepts related to validity assessment, including methods for establishing the accuracy of validity measures, and the importance of considering factors other than disability exaggeration that may contribute to failed validity measures.

Chapter 3 describes some of the most frequently used PVTs and SVTs and the format and typical duration of administration. Chapter 3 also describes the populations for which each test has been validated as well as populations for which their use may be problematic.

Chapter 4 will describe the practical application of incorporating validity measures in an assessment, how to integrate the results of validity measures with other assessment data, and how validity measure results can be incorporated in drawing conclusions from an assessment. Chapter 4 will also review a number of different influences on self-report measures, such as somatization, that should be considered when evaluating validity measures.

Summary

The current chapter introduced the concept of invalid responding in psychological and neuropsychological assessment and described some of the contexts in which this may occur. Different forms of invalid responding were described, including overreporting and underreporting of symptoms, which may be detected by Symptom Validity Tests (SVTS), as well as underperforming on cognitive or other measures, which may be detected by Performance Validity Tests (PVTs).

Chapter 2

Theoretical Underpinnings

In this chapter we will review theories related to validity assessment, including the conceptual basis for some of the different validity assessment methods. This chapter will introduce two frameworks that have been developed, one for the detection of malingered neurocognitive dysfunction (MND; Sherman et al., 2020; Slick et al., 1999) and the other for the detection of malingered pain-related disability (Bianchini et al., 2005). Both of these will be elaborated in more detail in Chapter 4. We will also introduce classification accuracy, which indicates how well different validity measures perform, and provides estimates of how likely it is that an examinee provided invalid assessment data.

Although we will review the rationale and methods by which the MND and MPRD allow for malingering-related diagnoses, it is important to keep in mind that validity measures are not used solely to divide examinees into "malingering" and "nonmalingering" categories. There are a number of factors other than malingering that can still result in assessment data that are not valid for interpretation. These can include an examinee's unwillingness to cooperate or lack of understanding of the nature of the assessment, confusion, sedating medications, as well as psychological factors such as somatization. These factors may cause an examinee to respond inconsistently, excessively slowly, or to overstate the number and severity of physical complaints, causing some or all of the assessment data to misrepresent the examinee. However, invalid data resulting from these factors would not be considered malingering.

The next section will review components of the MND and MPRD malingering frameworks in order to describe the different types of information to be gathered as part of the assessment process and how these data are evaluated to determine whether the assessment results should be considered an accurate characterization of the examinee.

Frameworks for Detecting and Diagnosing Malingering: MND and MPRD

The first system to formally assign a diagnosis of malingered neurocognitive dysfunction (MND) was published in 1999 (Slick et al., 1999), for which an updated version was recently published (Sherman et al., 2020). Bianchini and colleagues extended principles from the MND diagnostic framework to develop a diagnostic system for diagnosing malingered pain-related disability (MPRD; Bianchini et al., 2005). These diagnostic frameworks are important because they specify the forms of evidence that contribute to drawing conclusions about whether malingering is involved in an assessment, and provide differing levels of certainty (e.g., possible, probable, or definite malingering) based on validity measure results, as well as other forms of information.

Both the MND and MPRD incorporate self-report data, performance data, information from collateral sources (e.g., family members), and records, and evaluate the degree to which such information indicates intentional disability exaggeration. Within the MND and MPRD frameworks, "response bias" refers to indications that performance on well-validated measures of exaggeration of cognitive deficits is consistent with feigning. The MPRD introduced the concept of "effort bias", which refers to evidence of intentionally feigned impairment on measures of physical capacity (e.g., functional capacity evaluation). Both frameworks will be elaborated in more detail in Chapter 4, but their components will be briefly introduced in the following section.

Malingered Neurocognitive Dysfunction (MND)

The MND criteria allow for a conclusion that an examinee has malingered when there is sufficient evidence of "volitional exaggeration or fabrication of cognitive dysfunction and the absence of plausible alternative explanations" (Slick et al., 1999 p. 552). The evidence that contributes to these conclusions may come from self-report data, performance on cognitive measures, behavioral observation, records, and collateral reports.

The MND criteria assign differing levels of certainty that malingering has occurred based on the strength of evidence from the validity-related data, allowing for the diagnostic categories of Definite MND, Probable MND, and Possible MND. *Definite MND* (i.e., the examinee was definitely malingering) may be diagnosed when there is a finding of "definite negative response bias", which is generally defined as performing worse than chance on a force-choice cognitive measure. Given that simply guessing on a two-alternative forced-choice measure should result in approximately 50 % accuracy, if an examinee were to perform even worse than guessing (i.e., statistically significantly below 50 %), this would mean that the examinee identified the correct response and actively chose the incorrect response. In the context of a disability evaluation, this serves as an indication of intentional underperformance and may result in the examinee being classified as Definite MND (Slick et al., 1999).

An examinee may be classified as *Probable MND* when there is evidence of volitional disability exaggeration or fabrication, typically in the form of failing two or more well-validated validity measures, at least one of which must be performance-based (PVT). Instead of below-chance performance on forced-choice PVTs, "below cutoffs" on a PVT indicates that the examinee has performed significantly lower on the validity measure than nearly all individuals with the same or worse pathology. Other forms of evidence of feigning include discrepancies between test data and known patterns of brain functioning (e.g., performing in the average range on verbal memory testing but in the severely impaired range on measures of verbal attention); as well as discrepancies between test data and observed behavior (e.g., an examinee who exhibits normal conversational speech during an interview but performs in the severely impaired range on measures of verbal fluency).

Self-report data can also contribute to a diagnosis of probable MND, including inconsistences between self-reported history and documented history, between self-reported symptoms and known patterns of brain functioning (e.g., claims of extensive loss of autobiographical memory but with detailed memory of the mild head injury with no loss of consciousness) (e.g., Larrabee et al., 2007; Larrabee, 2012a). Other factors that contribute to the diagnosis of probable MND include discrepancies between self-reported symptoms and behavioral observations, such as complaints of significant memory complaints while demonstrating detailed recall of recent medical visits; and evidence from well-validated validity scales that indicate exaggerated or fabricated psychological, neuropsychological, or other forms of distress or dysfunction (Larrabee et al., 2007; Larrabee, 2012a).

Malingered Pain-Related Disability (MPRD)

Modeled after the MND criteria, the scope of malingering detection was extended to detect malingering associated with pain-related disability. The MPRD (Bianchini et al., 2005) framework is similar to the MND framework in the integration of information from multiple sources. However, the MPRD framework differs in emphasizing the detection of impairment that the individual attributes to the claimed pain-related condition, rather than the exaggeration of cognitive problems. In addition, the MPRD framework draws from additional sources of information including data from physical evaluation. The MPRD framework was also designed so that feigning of disability could be detected across physical, psychological/emotional, and cognitive functional domains.

Validity Detection: Principles and Strategies

The strategies and validity measures used by the MND and MPRD to detect feigned impairment or symptoms are based on a variety of principles. These may involve the way that the examinee performs on tasks, the symptoms that they self-report, as well as inconsistencies in their presentation. This section will describe the principles by which validity measures are developed.

Detecting Invalid Performance

Methods for detecting feigned or otherwise invalid performance on cognitive measures as discussed in Rogers et al. (1993) include *floor effects, performance curve,* and *performance validity testing* (although the term "Symptom validity testing" was used in the referenced paper, the term "performance validity testing" has become standard when the measure involves task performance rather than symptom endorsement). In addition, inconsistencies related to the examinee's performance on neuropsychological testing may serve as evidence of feigning if not explained by other factors.

The floor effect strategy is based on an examinee failing tasks that even severely impaired individuals would be able to successfully complete, such as very simple questions (e.g., "which is bigger, a horse or a dog?") (Rogers et al., 1993). Examinees who are attempting to feign cognitive impairment may answer incorrectly if they assume that appearing impaired requires that they make errors on such tasks. The 15-Item Memory Test (e.g., Lezak, 2012) is a measure that relies on the floor effect, as the actual memory demands are so low that even significantly impaired individuals are able to complete the tasks relatively easily. As such, individuals with less significant injuries who perform poorly on the 15-Item Test are presumed to be performing below their abilities to appear impaired.

The term "performance curve" takes advantage of the tendency for some feigning examinees to indiscriminately fail easy items as often as they fail more difficult items. Examinees who provide normal effort will produce a performance curve with better performance on easy items than more difficult items. As such, feigning disability may be detected when an examinee fails as many easy as difficult items. Although not always referred to by the term "performance curve", an examinee failing to recognize several items that they had successfully recalled within the same delay period would be inconsistent with the well-established principle that recognition is an easier task than recall.

Although the terminology has evolved over time, early validity measures referred to as Symptom Validity Tests (SVTs) consisted of two-alternative forced-choice tasks in which an examinee was asked to indicate whether their hand was touched by one finger or two (tactile SVTs; e.g., Greve et al., 2005), which of two visually presented digit strings they had previously heard, (auditory memory SVTs; e.g., Portland Digit Recognition Test [PDRT]; Binder, 1993a), or which of two line-drawn objects they had previously seen (visual memory SVTs; e.g., Test of Memory Malingering [TOMM]; Tombaugh, 1996). As noted earlier, these tasks would currently be called PVTs, although current PVTs are not limited to forced-choice tasks.

A strength of the force-choice tasks as validity measures is that the two-alternative format is associated with the binomial distribution; whereas an individual with no knowledge of the correct answer would be expected to perform approximately at chance (50 % correct in the case of a two-alternative format), an examinee who performed significantly worse than chance would have to identify and avoid the correct response repeatedly (Binder et al., 2014). This "below-chance" performance on a forced-choice PVT is considered the closest to an "evidentiary 'gold standard' for malingering" other than the examinee actually admitting to feigning (Slick et al., 1999, p. 551).

Whereas below-chance PVT serves as sufficiently strong evidence that a diagnosis of definite malingering (MND or MPRD) may be assigned, below-chance performance is relatively uncommon (Greve, Binder, & Bianchini 2009). A more frequent indication of feigned disability is "below cutoffs" performance on a PVT. "Below cutoffs" refers to performance that is worse than (below) some cutoff score that is usually established by identifying the lower range of scores produced by genuine patients with significant neurological injuries. Although the "below cutoffs" term has been used to distinguish it from "below chance" performance on a forced-choice PVT, "below cutoffs" is in fact the general basis for using most PVTs, regardless of their format (e.g., Greve, 2004).

Detecting Invalid Symptom Reporting

SVTs are used to detect feigning related to exaggeration or fabrication of symptoms, deficits, or other problems, either through responses on self-report measures or through clinical interview. SVTs take advantage of the principle that the individual involved in feigning is not able to draw from current personal experience of the psychological condition or problems they are trying to feign. For example, someone trying to appear psychotic but with no history of hallucinations or delusions would not be able to accurately report the lived experience of such symptoms. And even someone with a previous history of depression, who is not currently depressed, would have some difficulty accurately recalling the inner experience of the depressive episode after the condition had resolved.

Because of their lack of access to the lived experience of these symptoms, individuals attempting to present themselves as having a psychological disorder or as having some set of symptoms that they believe will further their goals (e.g., to be found not competent to stand trial, or to receive disability compensation) generally have to rely on their own understanding of what such a condition is like, and what sorts of symptoms or experiences they should report. Overreporting scales leverage the fact that most people without a condition are inaccurate in their estimation of which symptoms occur in different conditions, as well as the frequency, number, and duration of such symptoms. Validity scales are generally based on items characterized as "atypical responses", "infrequent responses", "rare symptoms" or "unusual combinations". In developing such scales, researchers would typically administer a measure to samples of patients with different psychological conditions (e.g., major depressive disorder, schizophrenia), and examine which items such patients tend to endorse, and which they rarely endorse. Items that appear to reflect psychopathology but are actually rarely endorsed by patients with verified psychopathology may be included in overreporting validity scales.

The MMPI in particular includes a number of different validity scales based on an infrequent responses principle. The F (Infrequency) scale consists of items rarely endorsed in the keyed direction by the standardization sample. The Fp (Infrequency Psychopathology) scale consists of items ostensibly reflecting psychopathology but that are rarely endorsed in the keyed direction by genuine patients with severe psychopathology. Elevated scores on either of these measures are associated with exaggerated psychological dysfunction. The MMPI FBS and RBS validity scales are based on endorsement of unusual combinations, with an elevated FBS associated with noncredible endorsement of somatic and/or cognitive symptoms, while an elevated RBS is associated with noncredible memory complaints (Ben-Porath & Tellegen, 2008; Ben-Porath & Tellegen, 2020).

Putting Validity Measures to the Test

Regardless of the underlying principles used to develop a PVT or SVT, the validity measure must be evaluated empirically to examine how well it performs in detecting feigning while simultaneously ensuring that honest responders with a variety of medical and psychiatric conditions are not mistakenly classified as feigning. The research methods used to test the effectiveness of validity measures are described in the next section.

Research Designs for Evaluating Validity Measures

In order to establish how well a measure performs in detecting feigned disability, researchers compare the performance on one or more measures of a group consisting of individuals known to be providing honest responses or genuine effort (often labeled as "nonmalingering", "honest", or "genuine") with the performance of a "feigning" (or "malingering") group consisting of individuals known or presumed to be feigning disability .

Because feigning inherently involves deception, forming groups that include individuals who are feigning disability can be challenging. The three most commonly used methods are (a) simulator (simulated disability) design; (b) criterion groups (known groups) design; and (c) differential prevalence design (Institute of Medicine[U.S.], 2015).

Simulator Group Design

Forming two or more groups of people and instructing one of the groups to simulate (fake) some sort of condition while instructing another group to respond honestly allows test developers and researchers to identify items or scales that differentiate honest responding from responding intended to feign having a condition. One advantage of this approach is that the researcher knows that invalid performance (feigning) was present in one group and not the other. A disadvantage of this approach is that the volunteer participants in simulator studies are often samples of convenience, such as college students or personnel at medical facilities, and so are often less representative of those who may be completing the measure in real world settings. Similarly, the way that research volunteers complete the measure in a research setting, even when instructed to feign disability, may be significantly different from the ways that actual examinees in settings that involve potentially significant outcomes (e.g., competency hearings, disability cases).

Criterion Groups (Known Groups) Design

A criterion groups design involves establishing clearly defined groups that differ on a variable of interest. In validity scale studies this would involve establishing at least one group known to have provided valid responses during assessment, and at least one group known to have responded in an invalid manner. Some researchers have formed feigning groups by using one of the malingering diagnosis frameworks described earlier (MND; Slick et al., 1999; MPRD; Bianchini et al., 2005). A valid group may be formed by selecting patients who had no incentive to appear impaired, or patients who may have had incentive to appear impaired but who had passed other well-established validity scales. Although some studies may include data from healthy examinees with no incentive to appear impaired, it is important to include patients with objectively established conditions in at least one of the valid samples. This is because the presence of different conditions may contribute to increases or decreases in scores on different validity scales, and so it is important to ensure that validity scale scores are calibrated so that variables other than invalid responding are considered and controlled for.

Differential Prevalence Design

A differential prevalence design is utilized in which a no-incentive group is compared with a disability-seeking group with known incentive to appear disabled. The assumption is that although not all members of the disability-seeking group are feigning, significantly more will be feigning than in the no-incentive group, and differences on the validity measure of interest may be examined.

Necessity of Criterion Groups Design

Although initial attempts to develop and evaluate a validity measure may rely on such imprecise methods as differential prevalence and simulator groups, in order to ensure a high level of accuracy in differentiating feigning from legitimate performance, researchers must develop well-defined criterion groups that include a clearly feigning group, as well as a group of clearly legitimate patients. Importantly, the legitimate patient group must include patients who have conditions that are likely to be present in contexts in which the validity measure is to be used. This is important because different medical, psychiatric, and neurological conditions may have effects on the validity measure that could overlap with the feigning group. For example, although most neurological conditions have little or no effect on performance on the TOMM, a limited number of conditions associated with significant memory impairment, such as Alzheimer's dementia, do reduce TOMM performance to a degree that would be misconstrued as feigned disability if the possibility of Alzheimer's dementia or similar conditions were not considered (e.g., Teichner & Wagner, 2004). As such, comparison groups must include patients with a range of relevant conditions so that the effects of these conditions on validity measure performance may be characterized. This type of research allows us to establish the classification accuracy of a measure.

Of course, not all possible conditions may have been sampled in the course of evaluating the classification accuracy of the validity scale, and it is important for professionals who are evaluating patients to consider whether a validity scale would be appropriate for use with a given patient. As such, with the selection of neuropsychological instruments, validity measures should be selected that are appropriate for the examinee's background and for the assessment context, and validity measure results should be interpreted with examinee limitations in mind. For example, because some patients with Alzheimer's dementia may be unable to comprehend some questions or accurately recall some information, it would be inappropriate to interpret a failed validity measure as indicating symptom overreporting when it may instead reflect Alzheimer's-related comprehension impairment. However, it should be noted that such comprehension difficulties would likely result in inconsistent responding as well, which would be detected by validity scales that detect excessive inconsistencies, such as the VRIN-r scale of the MMPI-2-RF.

Classification Accuracy

A perfect validity scale would always detect feigning or underreporting when it occurred and never classify someone as feigning or underreporting when they were responding honestly. However, because there are currently no perfect validity scales, there will always be cases in which a validity scale score points to an inaccurate conclusion. For example, if guidelines for a validity scale indicate that a score of 80 or above should be interpreted as indicating feigning, there may be cases in which an examinee who is attempting to respond honestly ends up with a score of 82. This would be considered a *false positive* error. Conversely, someone who was deliberately feigning at most points during an assessment may still respond in such a way that their validity scale score is a 75, below the cutoff value of 80. This would reflect a *false negative* error, or a "miss". When a validity measure accurately classifies as "valid" an examinee whose responses are honest, this would be considered a "true negative" classification (i.e., not feigning disability). If scores on a validity measure accurately detect that an examinee has feigned symptoms or impairment, this would be a "true positive". Table 1 describes the two types of correct and two types of incorrect classifications that can be made by a validity measure.

Table 1. Classification accuracy terms: Conclusion from validity measure score

Test Classification	Actually Feigning	Actually Valid
Feigning	True positive (Hit)	False negative (Miss)
Valid	False positive	True negative

Sensitivity and Specificity

As Table 1 illustrates, there are two ways that a test score can be right, and two ways that a test score can be wrong. The terms "Sensitivity" and "Specificity" quantify the accuracy of a validity measure at a given score. Sensitivity refers to the proportion of feigning examinees who were correctly classified as feigning using a given cutoff score (true positives) and may be expressed as a percentage. For example, if 70 out of 100 individuals known to be feigning scored 80 or higher on a validity measure with a cutoff score of 80 or above, the validity measure would have a sensitivity of 70 % at this cutoff score.

Sensitivity indicates the percentage of people with a certain characteristic who are accurately classified by the test at a particular cutting score as having that characteristic.

Conversely, specificity refers to the proportion of valid (honest) examinees who were correctly classified as responding honestly (true negatives). If 95 out of 100 valid responders scored below the cutoff score of 80 on the same validity measure just described, that measure would have 95 % specificity at this cutoff score.

Specificity indicates the percentage of people who do not have a certain characteristic who are accurately classified by the test as not having that characteristic.

Examining Figure 1, you will see that there are two sets of hypothetical distributions of scores on a validity scale. The distribution of scores to the left represent the "honest" responders, while the distribution of scores to the right represent the "feigning" or invalid responders. Although the average scores, represented by the highest point for each of the two distributions, are clearly different, we can see that there is an area where the scores of the "honest" group overlaps with scores of the "feigning" group. This means that scores within this range could be from someone either in the "feigning" group or the "honest" group. This also implies that there is no cutoff score that we could select that would avoid making one type of error or another: if the cutoff score for detecting feigning is set higher, there will be more false negative (miss) errors, such that feigning examinees will not be identified as feigning. If the cutoff score for detecting feigning is set lower, there will be more false positive errors, such that honest responders will be inaccurately classified as feigning. Although both types of error are undesirable, in certain contexts one type of error will be less undesirable than the other.

Using Figure 1 to illustrate, consider an example in which a sample of 100 examinees is known (by some gold standard) to be feigning a psychological condition (the "feigning" group). The distribution of scores for this feigning

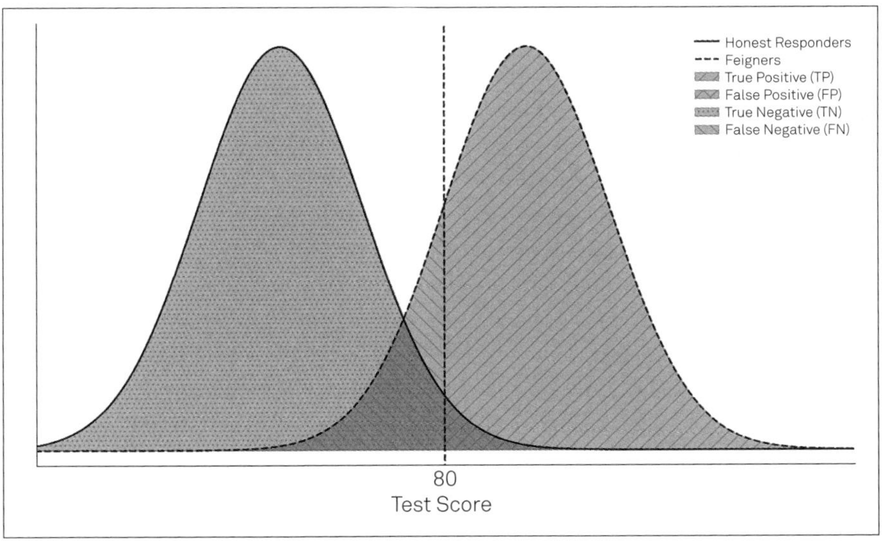

Figure 1. Illustration of sensitivity and specificity at a given test score.

group is on the right in the Figure. A second sample of 100 examinees is known to have responded honestly on the same test (the "honest" group), and the distribution for the honest group is on the left. Because the two distributions overlap, there is no cutoff score that could perfectly differentiate between the "honest" and "feigning" groups with perfect accuracy. However, we can use this information to decide what kinds of inaccuracies are more important and establish a cutoff score (or range of cutoff scores) and then quantify the degree of accuracy (and inaccuracy) associated with each cutoff score. Sensitivity and specificity are the variables that quantify two aspects of classification accuracy, measuring the percentage of those in the feigning group who are correctly classified as feigning (sensitivity), and the percentage of those who are not feigning who are correctly classified as not feigning (specificity).

It is important to note that sensitivity and specificity are not fixed values for a given validity measure. Rather, there would be different sensitivity and specificity values associated with different cutoff scores. For example, we could use lower cutoff scores in an effort to increase the percentage in the feigning group detected as feigning (i.e., to increase the sensitivity). We might find that at a cutoff score of 75 or above, 70 % of feigners were accurately detected as feigning (70 % sensitivity), and at a score of 70 or above, 85 % of feigners were detected (85 % sensitivity).

It may seem as though simply setting lower scores would be the best way to use this validity scale. However, the increase in the sensitivity that comes with using lower cutoff scores involves a tradeoff: as sensitivity increases with changes in the cutoff scores, the specificity at that cutoff score will typically be lower. This tradeoff involves a greater number of true positives accompanied by an increase in false positive errors. In the context of disability-related evaluations there has been a consensus that it is much more important to minimize false positive errors in order to avoid the negative consequences to a single individual falsely labeled as malingering; this requires setting cutoff scores in such a way as to maintain high specificity. A specificity of 90 % or above for any given measure is a widely accepted standard for validity measures (e.g., Greve, 2004). Setting a cutoff score for each individual validity scale reduces the likelihood of a false positive error, while administering several different validity measures within an assessment improves the overall ability to detect feigning.

In the next chapter we will review some of the most commonly used validity measures, including information about their sensitivity and specificity.

Chapter 3
Review of Commonly Used Validity Measures

This chapter will provide a review of some of the most commonly used and studied validity measures in neuropsychological and psychological assessments involving claims of impairment or disability. Far more validity measures have been developed than could be reviewed in the current chapter; however, the measures that surveys indicate are most frequently used in practice are included. The validity measures will generally be grouped together as performance validity tests (PVTs), which detect underperformance on tasks; and symptom validity tests (SVTs), which detect invalid self-reports such as symptom overreporting or endorsement of implausible symptoms or problems. Although most SVTs are based on self-report items, some standardized clinical interviews such as the SIRS and M-FAST have been developed to detect symptom invalidity.

A Note on Psychometric Properties of Validity Scales

It is standard practice in describing psychological measures to provide information about their psychometric properties, including different forms of reliability and validity. For most measures this is important because these properties describe the precision with which the measure assesses the construct of interest (reliability), and the extent to which the measure is appropriate for making inferences about the construct of interest for certain groups of examinees in particular situations.

The relevant psychometric properties of validity scales differ somewhat because the constructs that validity scales measure are not stable features of the examinee, but rather are indicators of whether the examinee responded consistently and in an accurate, forthright manner during testing. Although psychometric properties such as test-retest reliability are useful indicators of measures of stable constructs such as personality traits, we would not necessarily expect someone to produce the same validity scale scores across two time points (test-retest reliability) because the inattentiveness, low motivation, or lack of cooperation that were detected by the validity scale would not reflect a stable feature of the individual.

The more relevant indicators of accuracy for validity scales are Sensitivity and Specificity, which were introduced in Chapter 2. To recap, in the context of validity scales, sensitivity refers to the proportion of individuals providing invalid responses who are correctly classified by the test score as providing invalid responses. Specificity refers to the proportion of individuals who are responding in a valid manner who are correctly classified as such. The sensitivity and specificity of a validity measure depend in part on the nature of the groups being evaluated, because different populations may perform differently on the same measure. For example, the specificity of the TOMM at well-established cutoffs for samples without dementia is greater than 95%; that is, more than 95% of these examinees who respond to the best of their ability during testing will score in the valid range on the TOMM (i.e., will "pass" the TOMM). However, when patients with Alzheimer's disease are administered the TOMM, a significant percentage will score below cutoff scores and in the invalid range, classifying their performance as feigning impairment despite trying their best. This means that the TOMM has lower specificity when administered to Alzheimer's patients (Teichner & Wagner, 2004). At the same time, most neurological conditions other than Alzheimer's disease do not contribute to failure on PVTs. In the review of validity measures below, sensitivity and specificity values reported may exclude Alzheimer's patients or other conditions that would otherwise be associated with unacceptably high false positive errors.

Performance Validity Tests (PVTs)

Free-Standing Measures

The following section describes some of the most commonly used free-standing PVTs. The review is not comprehensive but includes the most frequently administered PVTs (Young et al., 2016) and indicates populations for which they have been validated, languages in which they may be administered, and the format in which they are administered. Because of concerns about test security, details about the measures that would allow them to be easily identified by examinees or that would allow examinees to tailor their performance are excluded.

Test of Malingering (TOMM)

The TOMM (Tombaugh, 1996) is one of the most widely used PVTs in psychological or neuropsychological assessments for disability-related claims (Martin et al., 2015; Young et al., 2016). Patients with a wide range of psychiatric and neurological conditions perform normally on the TOMM when they provide good effort, whereas individuals identified as malingering, and volunteer participants instructed to feign impairment produce significantly lower scores on the TOMM.

The TOMM involves the examiner presenting line drawings of common objects, one at a time, after which each of the drawings is presented along with a drawing of an object that was not previously seen. The examinee is asked to recognize the previously seen object and is told whether each response is correct or incorrect. Two trials are administered consecutively. After a 15-minute delay, the Retention trial is administered in which examinees are again asked to recognize the previous items. Some additional details of TOMM administration are withheld for test security.

The TOMM produces three separate scores, reflecting the total number of responses correct for each Trial 1, Trial 2, and the Retention Trial. Whereas the originally published guidelines set performance of <90% accuracy for Trial 2 or the Retention Trial as indicating invalid effort, subsequent research has demonstrated that sensitivity can be increased while maintaining excellent specific by setting higher cutoff scores. In a meta-analysis of 60 studies of the classification accuracy of the TOMM (Martin et al., 2020), it was determined that a cutoff score well above 90% on Trial 2 and the Retention Trial improved sensitivity (0.59–0.70) while still maintaining specificity sufficient to minimize false positive errors (0.91–0.97). The meta-analysis included studies in which Trial 1 of the TOMM had also been validated as a PVM, with a finding that a cutoff of <84% accuracy on Trial 1 resulted in good sensitivity (0.59–0.70) with specificity at or above 0.90 (Martin et al., 2020).

The TOMM has been found to have good sensitivity in detecting invalid effort, while maintaining high specificity, for patients claiming impairment due to concussion, traumatic brain injury (TBI), chronic pain complaints, depression, PTSD, and other psychiatric conditions including schizophrenia (Duncan, 2005). However, for a group of patients with low intellectual ability a lower cutoff for Trial 1 was needed to maintain adequate specificity (Smith et al., 2014). In addition, patients with Alzheimer's dementia tend to fail standard TOMM cutoffs at high rates, with specificity for Trial 2 of the TOMM ranging from 24% to 82% (Dean et al., 2009). As such, the TOMM likely should not be used if Alzheimer's dementia is known or suspected to be present.

Age: The TOMM was normed for ages 17–90, but has demonstrated adequate classification accuracy with examinees as young as 5 years of age (Constantinou & McCaffrey, 2003).

Administration Time: Approximately 15 minutes of administration, with a 15-minute interval between Trial 2 and Retention Trial.

Languages: Because the TOMM does not involve word stimuli it can be administered in any language.

Word Memory Test (WMT)

The WMT (Green, 2003) presents word stimuli on a computer screen with instructions for the examinee to remember the words. Although the number of words to be remembered exceeds memory capacity, the ability to associate separate words as familiar phrases reduces task difficulty such that performance relies more on effort than memory ability. Words are presented more than once to facilitate learning, followed by an immediate recognition trial and delayed recognition trial 30 minutes later. The recognition trials are essentially insensitive to most forms of genuine memory impairment and are much more sensitive to effort. Additional WMT tasks that may be affected by genuine memory impairment include a multiple-choice recognition task, a paired associates trial, a free recall trial, and after an additional 20-minute delay, a long delayed free recall trial.

The free recall trials are generally the most difficult and most affected by genuine memory impairment. As such, examining the results of the recall trials along with the easier trials allows the examiner to consider whether apparently invalid performance on some trials is more consistent with invalid effort or with a genuine memory impairment, such as Alzheimer's dementia. Although details of interpretation of these patterns are withheld for test security purposes, an advantage of the WMT is the inclusion of tasks that are differentially sensitive to memory impairment as well as effort. This results in the Genuine Memory Impairment Profile (GMIP) for each examinee, based on a three-step process that relies on differences in subtest difficulty to distinguish performance patterns due to true memory impairment from invalid performance (e.g., Alverson et al., 2019).

Age: The WMT has been validated for administration in children as young as 7 (Green & Flaro, 2003) and adults at least 80 years of age.

Administration Time: Total administration time for the WMT is approximately 20 minutes, not including the 30-minute delay from immediate recognition to delayed recognition, or the 20-minute delay for the optional long-delay free recall trial.

Languages: The publisher's website (Green, n.d.) for the WMT (https://wordmemorytest.com/languages/) lists 17 languages for which the WMT may be administered: Arabic, Danish, Dutch, English, Farsi, French, German, Greek, Hebrew, Italian, Japanese, Mandarin, Portuguese, Punjabi, Russian, Spanish, and Turkish.

Medical Symptom Validity Test (MSVT)

The MSVT (Green, 2004) is essentially a shorter version of the WMT, with half the number of word pairs as the WMT, with 4 subtests rather than 6, and with a shorter delay of 10 minutes between immediate and delayed subtests. These features allow the MSVT to be administered more quickly than the WMT, reducing overall administration time.

Like the WMT, some subtests of the MSVT are sensitive to feigning while insensitive to cognitive impairment, while other subtests are actually sensitive to significant memory impairment. This allows the MSVT to differentiate more accurately between poor performance that is attributable to feigning from poor performance attributable to significant memory dysfunction, as in dementia. The MSVT manual includes an algorithm based on patterns of memory performance to differentiate likely feigned performance from a genuine memory impairment. When using the algorithm, the specificity of the MSVT in early dementia (92%) and advanced dementia (89%) remained high (Green, 2004).

Ages: Adults, and children with at least a 3rd grade reading level.

Administration Time: The MSVT is administered by computer and takes approximately 5 minutes for the examinee to complete initial trials, with a 10-minute delay before completing delayed recognition, paired associate, and free recall trials, which take an additional 5 minutes.

Languages: The MSVT is available in English, Spanish, German, Dutch, Norwegian, Portuguese, and Danish.

Nonverbal Medical Symptom Validity Test (NV-MSVT)

The NV-MSVT (Green, 2008) is also related to the original WMT but is shorter and uses nonverbal stimuli to remember (drawings of objects) rather than words. Like the WMT and MSVT, the NV-MSVT is presented on computer and requires adequate visual acuity to be able to recognize the visual stimuli. Because of the nonverbal nature of the stimuli, the NV-MSVT does not require that the examinee be able to read.

The NV-MSVT involves four subtests that are sensitive to feigning, and two memory subtests that allow for profile analysis to distinguish failure due to severe cognitive deficits from failure due to invalid effort or feigning. This feature of being able to identify when validity failure is likely attributable to dementia or other severe cognitive deficits is similar to that of the WMT and MSVT and distinguishes these three PVTs from the other commonly administered PVTs. When examinee performance is evaluated by examining whether any failed validity subtest components are explained by performance on the memory subtests that matches the expected difficulty gradient (i.e., performing better on easier subtests than on more difficult subtests), the NV-MSVT reportedly reaches 70 % sensitivity while maintaining 100 % specificity (Sherman et al., 2023).

Age: Adults; children as young as 7 have been shown to perform with high accuracy.

Administration Time: The NV-MSVT is administered by computer and takes approximately 5 minutes for the examinee to complete initial trials, with a 10-minute delay before completing delayed memory tasks involving both recognition and recall, requiring an additional 5–10 minutes.

Languages: Publisher guidance (https://wordmemorytest.com/languages/) indicates that the NV-MSVT can be administered in any language because stimuli do not involve words, consisting only of drawn images (Green, n.d.), although is unclear whether cultural differences would reduce the specificity of the NV-MSVT in examinees from markedly different backgrounds.

Rey 15-Item Test (FIT)

The FIT (Boone, Salazar, et al., 2002; Rey, 1964) involves presentation of 15 items to be remembered, details of which are withheld for test security. Despite presentation of multiple items, the appearance and arrangement of the items allow for grouping in a way that imposes a much smaller memory load than 15 items. Examinees attempting to feign memory impairment likely overestimate the difficulty of the task and so will tend to perform poorly. Like the Dot Counting Test (Boone, Lu, et al., 2002), the FIT does not involve the two-alternative forced-choice format used in many PVTs, potentially making it less likely to be recognized as a validity measure.

A meta-analysis of the original version of the FIT indicated that it demonstrated high specificity but lower sensitivity than most PVTs (Reznek, 2005), although specificity was reduced in patients with intellectual disability. However, sensitivity was found to improve significantly when a recognition trial and modified scoring algorithm was developed. Using a cutoff score in which the FIT Total recalled score was added to a value consisting of the recognition true positive score minus false positive, sensitivity reached 70 % while maintaining specificity greater than 90 % (Boone, Salazar, et al., 2002).

Conditions: Nonlitigating patients with dementia (Dean et al., 2009) or intellectual disability (Marshall & Happe, 2007) tend to fail the FIT at unacceptably high levels (false positive errors); as such, the FIT should not be used if dementia is suspected or in examinees with known or suspected intellectual disability.

Age: Adults.

Administration Time: Approximately 5 minutes.

Languages: English and Spanish

Dot Counting Test

The Dot Counting Test (Boone, Lu, et al., 2002) involves presentation of arrays of dots, with the examinee instructed to count the number of dots on each array as quickly and accurately as they can. Scoring is based on a combination of accuracy and completion time. The Dot Counting Test is somewhat distinct from other PVTs in that it does not involve memory tasks. Although specific details are withheld for test security purposes, the Dot Counting Test tends to elicit performance patterns that differentiate those feigning disability from examinees with genuine cognitive impairment, based on analysis of both the speed and accuracy of task completion across the different types of dot arrays, with very good classification accuracy reported in English-speaking US samples (sensitivity of 60 % at specificity of 91.2 %; McCaul et al., 2018; Rhoads, Resch, et al., 2021). Some studies have found that using standard cutoff scores for the Dot Counting Test may result in reduced specificity in Eastern European examinees (Crişan & Sava, 2025) and in Spanish-speaking examinees living in the US (Rhoads, Leib, et al., 2021).

The Dot Counting Test has been validated for use in Spanish-speaking North American samples (Burton et al., 2012). Because the Dot Counting Test does not involve verbal material, it can likely be administered to non-English-speaking examinees if instructions are interpreted to be administered in their native language. However, significant cultural differences, especially lower education, may increase the risk of false-positive errors.

McCaul et al. (2018) reported that specificity was reduced in those with stroke and moderate dementia at the standard cutoff score but noted that cutoff scores could be adjusted for specific differential diagnoses. For examinees with intellectual disability, one study found that the cutoff score would need to be adjusted significantly to reach 90% specificity, at which point the sensitivity for detecting feigned intellectual disability was only 18% (Smith et al., 2014).

Age: 17 years old and above.

Administration Time: Approximately 10 minutes.

Languages: English, Spanish, and potentially other languages via interpretation of instructions.

Victoria Symptom Validity Test (VSVT)

The VSVT (Slick et al., 1997) is a two-alternative, forced-choice measure that is administered by computer. Tasks involve presentation of numbers to be remembered, with some items made to appear more difficult. In addition to scoring response accuracy, the program also records response time, and both may be used toward classifying performance as valid, invalid, or questionable. The original version was developed on the basis of binomial theory-based probability, with performance based on random guessing as a reference, rather than comparison to a normative sample.

Age: 18 years and above.

Administration Time: 15–20 minutes.

Language: English.

Embedded PVT Measures

Whereas most stand-alone PVTs are commercially published and must be purchased, embedded validity measures are included within standard neuropsychological tests. Even when additional stand-alone PVTs are administered, embedded PVTs increase the coverage of validity checks throughout an assessment. Substantial empirical support has accrued for the most frequently used embedded PVTs (Young et al., 2016) which include CVLT Forced-Choice errors (Delis et al., 2000), Reliable Digit Span (Greiffenstein et al., 1994), Wisconsin Card Sort Test Failure to Maintain Set (Greve, Heinly, Bianchini, & Love, 2009), Digit Span Age-Corrected Scale Score (Heinly et al., 2005), and RBANS Effort Index (Silverberg et al., 2007).

Administration and Scoring Details

Whereas the stand-alone PVTs require that the clinician purchase the manual or related documentation to administer the PVT, embedded PVTs have mostly been developed outside of the originally published neuropsychological measure. Because guidance for administering and scoring the stand-alone PVTs is detailed in the publisher documentation, withholding these details in the current book would not impede the reader's ability to implement the measures.

However, for embedded PVT measures, guidance on administration, scoring, and interpretation is more likely to be scattered across a variety of research papers not contained within the publisher's manual for the neuropsychological measure from which the embedded PVT was derived. As such, the utility of the current book requires striking a balance between maintaining the security of the validity measures against the need for clinicians to be able to correctly score the embedded PVTs and to interpret them appropriately considering published classification accuracy studies. For this reason, the embedded PVTs will include some information about scoring and interpretation while attempting to guard details that would allow an examinee to be coached in "passing" the embedded PVT.

California Verbal Learning Test, 2nd edition (CVLT-II) Forced Choice Recognition

The CVLT-II Forced Choice Recognition (FCR; Delis et al., 2000) trial is something of a hybrid between a stand-alone PVT and an embedded PVT because it was added on as a validity measure to a standard measure of verbal learning and memory. Because details of administering and interpreting the FCR are included in the user's manual, they are described only generally here. The FCR is administered after all other CVLT-II subtests have been administered, with a several-minute interval between the previous subtest and the FCR trial. Examinees are presented with pairs of words and are asked to identify which word was on the previously presented list. Accuracy on the FCR is high in the nonclinical normative sample and remains high in many neurological conditions.

A systematic review of the FCR found that using a cutoff score of ≤14 was associated with 50 % sensitivity while maintaining 93 % specificity (Schwartz et al., 2016). Samples with moderate-severe TBI were found to pass the FCR at high rates, with specificity rates around 97 % (Miller et al., 2011; Moore & Donders, 2004).

However, Alzheimer's dementia was associated with high FCR failure rates, meaning that the FCR would have low specificity for this population at the standard cutoff. Although patients with mild Alzheimer's dementia had a false positive error rate of 12.5 %, moderate Alzheimer's dementia was associated with a 71.4 % false positive error rate (Clark et al., 2012). As such, the FCR should not be utilized as a PVT for patients with known or suspected Alzheimer's dementia. However, specificity is relatively high for most other neurological conditions.

Age: 16–89 years (CVLT-II adult version); 5–16 years (CVLT-C children's version).

Languages: English and multiple translations.

Reliable Digit Span (RDS)

RDS (Greiffenstein et al., 1994) was developed based on observations of an unlikely pattern of errors during administration of the WAIS Digit Span test (Greiffenstein et al., 1994). RDS reflects the sum of the longest digit string for which full credit is earned on forward and backward conditions on the Digit Span subtest of Weschsler-based measures (WAIS, WISC). For adults, cutoff scores of ≤ 7 or ≤ 6 have typically been used; however, there are a number of neurological conditions for which a cutoff score of ≤7 has inadequate specificity and so raises concerns about false positive errors.

A systematic review of several RDS studies reported a weighted mean specificity of 82 % with weighted mean sensitivity of 48 %, when using a cutoff score of ≤7. (Schroeder et al., 2012). When a cutoff score of ≤6 was used, the weighted mean specificity was 96 %, with weighted mean sensitivity of 30 %.

However, certain conditions were excluded from these weighted mean values because they were associated with high false positive error rates. These included cerebrovascular accident and memory disorders (Heinly et al., 2005), and groups with IQ of 50–79 (Dean et al., 2008), for whom specificity rates were as low as 33%, even at the more stringent cutoff score of ≤6. As such, caution is necessary when using RDS with certain populations, as even the ≤6 cutoff may result in excessive false-positive rates in patients with severe memory disorders or intellectual disability. However, RDS performance was found to be relatively unaffected by depression (Larrabee, 2012a), pain conditions (Etherton et al., 2005), mild TBI (Heinly et al., 2005; Meyers & Volbrecht, 1998), or moderate to severe TBI (Larrabee, 2003a).

The RDS has also been found to have good classification accuracy in assessing performance validity in pediatric neuropsychological evaluations using the WISC digit span subtests. In a study involving 274 mild TBI patients 8 to 16 years of age, an RDS cutoff score of ≤6 was associated with sensitivity of 51% and 92% (Kirkwood et al., 2011).

Age: 8–90 years.

Languages: Available in languages for which Wechsler scales have been translated.

Repeatable Battery for the Assessment of Neuropsychological Status (RBANS) Effort Index (EI)

The RBANS (Rabin et al., 2005) Effort Index (EI; Silverberg et al., 2007) is an embedded validity indicator developed by Silverberg et al. (2007) that is derived from the Digit Span and List Recognition subtests of the RBANS. The Digit Span subtest is similar to that of the WAIS and WISC, requiring the examinee to repeat orally presented digit strings of increasing length. The List Recognition subtest involves identifying 10 previously presented items from distractor items by making old/new judgments.

The EI was created by assigning weights to Digit Span and List Recognition raw scores that occurred in bona fide clinical patients at varying frequencies (scoring details are from Silverberg et al., 2007). The following percentile ranges were used to assign weighted scores: 0, 0.1–1.9, 2–4.9, 5–8.9, 9–15.9, 16–24.9, and ≥25. Raw scores for Digit Span and for List Recognition that were at these percentile ranges were assigned weighted scores of 6, 5, 4, 3, 2, 1, and 0 respectively, such that the less commonly the score occurred in clinical patients with genuine cognitive impairment, the greater the weighted score. Summing the weighted scores for Digit Span and List Recognition produces the composite EI score. Specificity for the EI in a sample of mild TBI patients was 100 % when using a cutoff of EI >3, and 90.6 % when using a cutoff of EI >2 (Silverberg et al., 2007)

A systematic review of RBANS validity indicators (Shura et al., 2018) concluded that, for younger examinees with mild TBI, a cutoff of EI ≥1 is optimal, with good sensitivity while maintaining adequate specificity. However, with older examinees and for conditions more severe than mild TBI, a cutoff score of ≥3 may be necessary to avoid false positive errors (Shura et al., 2018).

Age: 12–89 years.

Languages: English and multiple translations available for RBANS.

Wisconsin Card Sort Test (WCST) Failure to Maintain Set (FMS)

Failure to Maintain Set (FMS; Heaton et al., 1993) is a standard component of the Wisconsin Card Sorting Test, indicating the number of times that an examinee completes five or more consecutive correct responses but then makes an error (fails to maintain set) before completing the category. Importantly, failure to maintain set (FMS) errors may occur at elevated rates in patients with ventromedial prefrontal cortex damage (Rickards et al., 2018), limiting its use for examinees with such injuries. However, FMS errors are otherwise relatively rare in both healthy individuals and in those with a variety of neurological conditions. As such, FMS errors in examinees without more severe pathology may reflect invalid performance.

Using a cutoff score of FMS errors ≥3, sensitivity of approximately 30 % was obtained with specificity ≥90 % in a mixed clinical sample (Greve et al., 2009). In a sample of children (7–17 years of age), it was found that FMS ≥3 likely resulted in too many false positive errors (Lichtenstein et al., 2018). The authors recommended FMS ≥4 to ensure adequate specificity when used to assess performance validity in children, although sensitivity was generally relatively weak (7–38 %) at this cutoff (Lichtenstein et al., 2018). An advantage of FMS errors compared with other PVTs is that it does not utilize the forced-choice recognition paradigm common to many PVTs and so is likely less easily identified as a validity measure.

Age: 6.5–89 years.

Languages: English and Spanish.

Self-Report and Interview-Based Symptom Validity Tests (SVTs)

MMPI-Based Validity Scales

Although the most recent version of the adult version of the MMPI (MMPI-3) was published in 2020, (Ben-Porath & Tellegen, 2020) the MMPI-2-RF and even the MMPI-2 continue to be used. Most of the validity scales from the MMPI-2 have persisted through subsequent editions, and the interpretive guidelines are generally the same across versions. The MMPI-2-RF and MMPI-3 include a number of validity scales added since the MMPI-2. Any additions or changes in validity measures or interpretive guidance across versions will be noted. For simplicity, the term MMPI will be used unless one of the versions is excluded.

Publisher guidelines caution that elevated scores on the overreporting validity scales do not specify whether the overreporting is intentional; however, elevated validity scales may be integrated with other sources of information to support or weaken conclusions about the possibility of intentional feigning or malingering (Ben-Porath, 2012).

When completing the MMPI, examinees may overreport psychological symptoms, physical/somatic symptoms, or cognitive symptoms; they may also endorse items rarely endorsed by others, which is interpreted as an attempt to feign pathology (Ben-Porath, 2012). While it is important to also consider whether the presence of a psychological condition may contribute to unintentional overreporting (e.g., examinees with somatic symptom disorder may endorse a high number of somatic complaints), the MMPI validity scale norms include individuals with a range of psychological disorders. As such, the presence of a psychological disorder alone would not fully explain a significantly elevated overreporting validity scale.

The following scales and guidance for interpreting each are based on interpretive manuals for the MMPI-2-RF (Ben-Porath, 2012) and the MMPI-3 (Ben-Porath & Sellbom, 2023). Earlier MMPI versions contain fewer validity scales, however, the interpretive guidance is the same as for the MMPI-2-RF and MMPI-3 for shared validity scales.

Infrequent Responses (F)

The F scale includes 35 items that were rarely endorsed in the normative sample. These items are not limited to a specific type of experience but include psychological, somatic, and cognitive symptoms. If the noncontent responding validity scales (CRIN, VRIN, and TRIN) indicate consistent responding, then an F scale elevation will suggest overreporting. Although F may be elevated somewhat by genuine distress or significant psychopathology, the higher the score, the greater the likelihood that the protocol reflects overreporting rather than psychological distress.

Infrequent Psychopathology Responses (Fp)

The Fp comprises 21 items that appear to reflect psychological symptoms but are rarely endorsed by individuals diagnosed with severe psychopathology. For this reason, the Fp is less likely to be elevated by emotional distress or psychopathology than the F scale, making the Fp more useful in detecting overreporting of psychological symptoms.

Infrequent Somatic Responses (Fs)

The Fs includes 16 items related to somatic symptoms that are infrequently endorsed by medical patients undergoing treatment for a range of medical conditions. Fs is intended to detect overreporting of somatic symptoms.

Fake Bad Scale (FBS)

The FBS (Lees-Haley et al., 1991) was initially developed for the MMPI-2 by Lees-Haley et al. (1991), who identified a number of somewhat disparate items that he found to differentiate individuals responding genuinely from those identified as feigning disability. The MMPI manual describes FBS elevations as reflecting "an unusual combination of responses that is associated with noncredible reporting of somatic and/or cognitive symptoms" (Ben-Porath & Sellbom, 2023, p. 349). Although some researchers initially challenged the utility of the FBS (e.g., Butcher et al., 2003), these initial objections were found to be inaccurate (Greve & Bianchini, 2004), and numerous subsequent studies have confirmed the utility of the FBS in detecting overreporting of somatic and cognitive symptoms as summarized in a 2010 meta-analysis (Nelson et al., 2010).

Response Bias Scale (RBS)

The Response Bias Scale (RBS; Gervais et al., 2007) is an embedded symptom validity indicator designed to identify exaggerated cognitive complaints, primarily memory complaints. The scale was developed by identifying items that discriminated between disability litigants who failed PVTs from those who passed. The RBS has demonstrated very good classification accuracy in civil forensic settings, and has been identified as one of the most effective SVTs in detecting feigned cognitive symptoms, with high sensitivity while maintaining very good specificity.

Age: 18–89 years.

Languages: English and multiple translations where MMPI-3 is available.

Structured Inventory of Malingered Symptomatology (SIMS)

The SIMS (Widows & Smith, 2005) is a 75-item self-report measure that is intended to screen for feigned or exaggerated psychological symptoms, cognitive impairment, and neurological complaints. The SIMS may be administered via paper response forms and pencil, or by computer, which generates computerized scoring output. The SIMS provides an overall score that serves as an index of feigning, as well as five subscales that indicate feigning in the specific domains of psychosis, neurological impairment, amnestic disorders, low intelligence, and affective disorders.

The SIMS total score ranges from 0 to 75, with higher scores indicating a greater probability of feigning. The SIMS scoring output provides guidance on scores for each subscale that are considered likely to reflect overreporting (specific cutoff scores are not reported here for test security), which indicates whether an examinee appears to be emphasizing a particular form of impairment.

In a meta-analytic review the SIMS had generally good classification accuracy in detecting feigning (Van Impelen et al., 2014), differentiating honest responders from a range of feigning simulators (Jelicic et al., 2007), disability claimants (Merten et al., 2009), and criminal defendants (Heinze & Purisch, 2001). However, feigning may be overestimated in examinees with schizophrenia or intellectual disability (Van Impelen et al., 2014). In addition, the authors of the meta-analysis (Van Impelen et al., 2014) suggested that original SIMS Total cutoff scores may have inadequate specificity. As such, users of the SIMS may wish to set higher cutoff scores for their examinees, particularly examinees with schizophrenia or intellectual disability.

> Administration Time: 10–15 minutes.
>
> Age: 18–99 years.
>
> Language: English.

Miller Forensic Assessment Test (M-FAST)

The M-FAST (Miller, 2001) is administered as a structured interview, consisting of 25 items intended to detect feigned psychopathology. Although the M-FAST total score has been identified as the most effective at distinguished feigning from honest responders, specific subscales are available, each intended to detect different types of feigning. The subscales include discrepancies between reported versus observed symptoms, extreme symptomatology, rare combinations, unusual hallucinations, unusual symptom course, negative image, and suggestibility (Miller, 2001). The M-FAST has been examined in both simulated psychopathology designs and known-groups clinical studies (Alwes et al., 2008; Vitacco et al., 2007).

Because the M-FAST is administered as a structured interview in which items are read by the clinician, it may be particularly appropriate for examinees who have difficulties with reading.

> Administration time: 5–10 minutes administration, 5 minutes for scoring.
>
> Age: 18–71 years.
>
> Language: English.

Chapter 4

Professional Issues in Validity Assessment

In this chapter we will describe approaches to planning how to select and incorporate validity measures within an assessment, and how to interpret validity measure results to make inferences about the meaning of assessment results. This chapter will also review a number of factors other than feigning that may affect the examinee's self-report, such as somatization, and ways to differentiate such nonfeigning factors from intentional feigning.

The chapter will begin with an overview of contexts in which feigning of impairment is more likely to occur, and a description of two diagnostic frameworks that have been developed to organize the methods and kinds of information used to detect feigned disability (i.e., MND and MPRD). Much of the rest of the chapter will involve steps involved in interpreting validity score results, considering nonfeigning explanations for anomalous validity measure scores, and reaching conclusions about the degree to which assessment results can be regarded as valid.

Disability Evaluations

Disability evaluations are among the most common situations for which systematic assessment of validity is essential. Disability claims may involve financial incentives to fabricate or exaggerate symptoms or deficits. Although in some cases the amount of incentive may involve wage replacement for a limited period of time involving a few thousand US dollars, in some jurisdictions the potential award may be uncapped, such that the potential award may involve millions of US dollars. It has been shown that the prevalence of disability-related malingering increases in proportion to the amount of the potential financial award (Bianchini et al., 2006). Given such incentives it is not surprising that some individuals would attempt to appear impaired in one or more ways.

Venues for Disability Claims

Claims for disability may be filed with US governmental agencies including the Social Security Administration, Veteran's Administration, state-administered Worker's Compensation agencies, and with civil courts for personal injury litigation. In addition, educational accommodations for claimed disabilities may be requested in primary school, college, and postgraduate settings. Although the nature of the proceedings differs among the different contexts, the methods and instruments used to assess validity are broadly the same.

Types of Impairment

Assessment batteries may differ significantly depending on the nature of the condition or impairment for which disability is claimed. For example, a claim for cognitive impairment due to a traumatic brain injury may involve extensive neuropsychological testing, whereas a claim involving PTSD attributed to a work-related assault would involve a more detailed trauma-related interview and self-report measures, with less emphasis on cognitive/neuropsychological testing. Later sections below review validity measures that are appropriate for most assessments for which impairment or disability is claimed, followed by measures more specifically applicable to claims involving different forms of impairment. The main functional domains in which disability may be claimed are described next.

Functional Domains Related to Disability

Three primary areas for which claimants may seek disability benefits include: 1. *Neurocognitive impairment,* 2. *Psychological impairment,* and 3. *Pain/physical impairment.* Neurocognitive impairment cases would include claims of problems with attention, concentration, working memory, and similar abilities. Psychological claims often involve alleged PTSD or depression. Pain/physical impairment cases may involve back pain, joint pain, or other musculoskeletal conditions, headaches, and numerous other complaints involving physical limitation or pain (e.g., Bianchini et al., 2005).

Although the type of impairment for which disability benefits are sought generally matches the nature of the injury (e.g., a traumatic brain injury patient would likely claim disability due to cognitive deficits), it is important to address whether the other domains may also be relevant to a claim. For example, a claim involving cognitive complaints may be influenced by preexisting psychological factors such as a somatic symptom disorder, such that the individual overstates the severity of the ostensible cognitive deficits. In addition, some examinees may pursue a higher disability award by feigning or exaggerating disability in more than one domain. For example, a person seeking disability benefits for cognitive deficits related to a motor vehicle accident may broaden the scope of their claim by feigning psychological impairment in the form of PTSD or depression. Similarly, someone pursuing a personal injury claim for a back injury from a slip and fall accident may attempt to broaden the degree of impairment by also claiming cognitive deficits due to pain, or psychological impairment due to depression caused by the pain, or both (Bianchini et al., 2005).

Variability in Approaches to Feigning Impairment

Examinees' attempts to feign impairment likely depend on their own perceptions of what it would mean to appear impaired, and how that should be manifested. As such, different examinees may perform normally on some validity scales while failing others. Because of this, it is recommended that examiners use a number of different types of validity measures across different domains. Using multiple validity measures across different domains is also important because the emphasis on setting cutoff scores at levels that minimize false positive errors means that there will likely be a significant number of false negative errors for each individual validity scale. For example, if a validity measure has specificity of 95% and sensitivity of 60% at a given cutoff score, this would mean that 5% of examinees with valid responses would be incorrectly classified as feigning (false positive errors), while 40% of feigning examinees would not be classified as feigning (false positive errors).

As described in Chapter 2, maintaining high specificity to avoid false positive errors involves a trade-off in the form of reduced sensitivity for any given validity measure. However, reduced sensitivity for each individual measure may be remedied by including several different validity measures, such that the likelihood of detecting feigning aggregated across all measures increases significantly. For example, one examinee may attempt to feign impairment by purposefully making errors on tasks involving memory, and so may fail the TOMM or WMT, but pass nonmemory-based PVTs such as the Dot Counting Test. Conversely, an examinee who has been coached to identify memory-based PVTs may avoid detection on the TOMM and WMT but may attempt to feign impairment through responding very slowly, potentially allowing for detection by the Dot Counting Test, which is not memory-based but detects feigning in part, on the basis of excessively long response times.

Of course, examinees will not volunteer what approach they are taking to feign impairment, or what type of PVTs they are aware of and trying to defeat; feigning impairment inherently involves withholding information and disguising one's intentions. The use of multiple PVTs with different formats improves the clinician's ability to detect feigning in the various manifestations in which it may appear.

The first systematic framework for integrating information related to assessment validity, establishing diagnostic criteria for detecting malingered neurocognitive dysfunction (MND), was published in 1999 (Slick et al., 1999). This framework was subsequently adapted and expanded into a framework for the diagnosis of malingered pain-related disability (MPRD; Bianchini et al., 2005). Although clinicians are not obligated to formally diagnose malingering or to label invalid test performance as malingering, these frameworks have been invaluable in organizing research related to the detection of feigned or exaggerated symptoms or deficits, and in the development and refinement of measures and strategies for detecting different forms of malingering. The next section provides an overview of the MND and MPRD and the principles and methods used in assessing symptom validity and performance validity, as well as drawing attention to the importance of considering competing explanations for presentations that might otherwise be interpreted as intentional feigning. Whether or not the diagnostic frameworks are used to formally diagnose malingering, the principles and methods used are important as empirically supported approaches to assessing validity.

Malingered Neurocognitive Dysfunction (MND)

The first formal framework for diagnosing malingered neurocognitive dysfunction was intended primarily to detect disability exaggeration in head injury claims (Slick et al., 1999). An updated version of the criteria was published in 2020 (Sherman et al., 2020), with modifications to some of the original criteria. The original framework was intended to identify specific, clearly defined criteria that incorporate several sources of information, including test-related observations as well as collateral information. Their framework also provided guidance on making differential diagnoses between malingering and other potential explanations for unusual or invalid presentations. The original (Slick et al., 1999) paper provided the following definition:

> Malingering of Neurocognitive Dysfunction (MND) is the volitional exaggeration or fabrication of cognitive dysfunction for the purpose of obtaining substantial material gain or avoiding or escaping formal duty or responsibility. Substantial material gain includes money, goods, or services of nontrivial value (e.g., financial com-

> pensation for personal injury). Formal duties are actions that people are legally obligated to perform (e.g., prison, military, or public service, or child support payments or other financial obligations). Formal responsibilities are those that involve accountability or liability in legal proceedings (e.g., competency to stand trial). (Slick et al., 1999, p. 552)

An update to the MND was published in 2020 with a number of modifications (Sherman et al., 2020). However, much of the published research on malingering detection used the original MND framework, and the original MND is emphasized in the current chapter.

The MND criteria are presented in the Appendix but will be summarized here. A diagnosis of MND requires the presence of a substantial and identifiable external incentive to appear impaired, and any findings that are interpreted as indicating exaggeration or fabrication of symptoms or deficits must not be attributable to other factors (e.g., intellectual disability, dementia).

Differing levels of certainty may be assigned to a diagnosis of MND. A diagnosis of *Definite* MND requires evidence of definite negative response bias, which is operationalized as "below-chance" performance on a forced-choice measure. The rationale for the use of below-chance performance to identify definite negative response bias is that, for any two-alternative forced-choice, simply guessing at the correct response with no knowledge of the correct answer would result in 50 % accuracy on average. Performing significantly worse than chance requires identifying and avoiding the correct response, which is considered to be evidence of intentional underperformance.

Diagnosing *Probable* MND requires either two or more findings from neuropsychological testing using well-validated PVTs that are consistent with probable response bias; discrepancies between test data and known patterns of brain functioning, observed behavior, reliable collateral reports, or background history; or one of these forms of evidence from neuropsychological test results and an additional form of evidence from self-report. The evidence from self-report can include discrepancies between self-report data and the areas described above (i.e., brain functioning, observed behavior, etc.), or from well-validated self-report symptom validity scales consistent with exaggeration or fabrication of psychological dysfunction.

The MND criteria refer to well-validated PVT measures and well-validated self-report instruments that have been established as effective in detecting feigning of cognitive impairment or feigning self-reported symptoms or deficits. Selecting PVTs and SVTs that have been thoroughly validated for use with a particular examinee is important for adequate validity assessment.

Using the MND Criteria in Practice

Although the MND criteria were developed initially for use with neuropsychological assessments and allow for a formal diagnosis of malingering, the principles and components of the MND, and the research findings from related research allow clinicians to assess for invalid presentations in settings other than neuropsychological assessments, and to do so without necessarily assigning a formal diagnosis of malingering. For example, when claims are related to a psychological condition without a neurological injury but with complaints of problems with concentration or memory, it would be appropriate to administer cognitive (neuropsychological) tasks in order to both assess these cognitive abilities, and also to assess performance validity. Digit span tasks from the WAIS, RBANS, and other standard measures may be administered to assess attention and working memory performance, while embedded validity measures may be derived from analysis of digit span performance to detect potential invalid performance.

Malingered Pain-Related Disability

Disability claimants with physical injury may feign or exaggerate symptoms or deficits that they attribute to the compensable injury. Following the framework developed by Slick et al. (1999) for the diagnosis of MND, Bianchini et al. (2005) published a framework for diagnosing malingered pain-related disability (MPRD). The MPRD criteria acknowledge a "multidimensional presentation of disability", as pain patients often report not only physical symptoms and impairment, but also psychological/emotional problems and cognitive deficits. The authors observed that, within some jurisdictions and disability venues, patients pursuing a disability claim have an incentive to appear impaired in a number of different ways, and as such they may feign or exaggerate symptoms or deficits in psychological and cognitive domains in addition to any physical limitations they may claim. As such, the MPRD diagnostic system incorporates validity-related information regarding physical, psychological, and cognitive domains.

The authors of the MPRD make the important point that the assessment process is not intended to address how much pain the claimant is experiencing, or whether a claimant is or is not injured, noting that claimants who are truly injured and who truly experience pain can also engage in malingering. Rather, the issue to be addressed involves whether the claimant is feigning or exaggerating the disability that they attribute to the injury or associated pain (Bianchini et al., 2005).

Clinical Pearl

Assessing MPRD involves assessing exaggeration of impairment attributed to pain and not detecting exaggeration of pain itself.

Like the MND, the MPRD describes differing levels of certainty about the presence of malingering: Definite, Probable, and Possible Malingering. As with the MND, the MPRD regards "below-chance" performance on forced-choice testing as evidence of intentional underperformance, because such performance requires identifying but avoiding the correct response. As such, below-chance failure on a forced-choice PVT is one finding that may allow designation of Definite Malingering.

Compelling Inconsistencies

In addition to specific SVT and PVT measures, evidence of "compelling inconsistencies" may permit a diagnosis of Definite Malingering in the MPRD system. A "compelling inconsistency" occurs when "the difference in the way a patient presents when being evaluated compared with when they are not aware of being evaluated is such that it is not reasonable to believe the patient is not purposely controlling the difference" (Bianchini et al., 2005, p. 408). A patient claiming during disability evaluation that they cannot work because of the effects of an injury or condition but who is at the same time found to be working in a physically demanding position would be demonstrating a compelling inconsistency that would indicate intentional disability exaggeration. This example provides a strong example of a compelling inconsistency because it is not plausible that the patient would be unaware of the discrepancy between claiming during a disability evaluation, that they could not work, while also working elsewhere in a demanding position. Other situations may be less obvious, such as someone who may be able to do light yard work at a slow pace but unable to perform the physically demanding tasks, fast-paced tasks required by his job. Such situations require a degree of clinical judgment in determining whether apparent discrepancies would actually represent a compelling inconsistency.

With the MND and MPRD frameworks as a background, the next section will discuss planning for an assessment involving claims of disability.

Planning for a Disability-Related Neuropsychological or Psychological Assessment

In addition to selecting psychological or neuropsychological tests and procedures to assess relevant functional domains and symptoms including specific impairments or deficits identified by the claimant or by physicians, or other evaluators, it is important to include a range of validity measures, both PVTs and SVTs, across the assessment battery. It is useful to sample validity at different time points during the assessment, because examinees may change their test-taking approach over the course of the assessment. For example, an examinee may perform normally on some tasks before deciding that they should underperform to appear impaired. Similarly, motivation and level of cooperation may vary across time resulting in fluctuating valid and invalid performance at different points in the assessment. Planning to administer validity measures at different times during the assessment allows for a more comprehensive picture of the degree to which the assessment data reflect genuine symptom report and valid effort.

Review of Records

Reviewing available records is a valuable element in assessment planning, typically providing information about the examinee's educational attainment, employment history, medical conditions, and psychological history, as well as information about the examinee's functioning prior to and following the index event. Some of the most important types of information that may be obtained from record reviews are described in this section.

Matching Examinee Characteristics to Appropriate Validity Measures

This is important for ensuring that the background characteristics of the examinee are appropriate for SVTs and PVTs that will be included in the assessment. For example, many PVTs are inappropriate for use with examinees who have moderate Alzheimer's dementia because this condition tends to produce a high number of false positive errors. PVTs that require fluent reading would be inappropriate for examinees who are unable to read. Reviewing records to determine whether validity measures are appropriate for the patient's characteristics will avoid wasted time in administering validity measures that cannot be accurately interpreted, or worse, ignoring such limitations and inappropriately interpreting obtained validity scores when the norms do not extend to the examinee.

Identifying Relevant Background Medical or Psychological Factors

Records may provide information about psychological or medical conditions that may influence the examinee's performance whether or not the examinee is aware of such influence. For example, obstructive sleep apnea is a relatively common condition that involves periods in which a person stops breathing for varying periods of time during sleep. The cessation in breathing may cause the person to wake or partially wake, causing disruption or even absence of deeper stages of sleep. Because the deeper stages of sleep are important for memory consolidation and for obtaining refreshing sleep, untreated obstructive sleep apnea may result in memory difficulties, reduced concentration, irritability, and fatigue, all of which may be misattributed to a minor head injury from which no persistent cognitive problems would be expected to occur.

Characterizing the Nature of the Index Event

It is important to attempt to obtain independent information about any injury, trauma exposure, or other relevant event that has been identified as causing or contributing to the condition or disability that led to the assessment. Examinees may misremember some elements of an event, may have no memory for a head injury involving a period of posttraumatic amnesia or loss of consciousness, or may intentionally misrepresent the nature of the event to increase the apparent severity of an injury or intensity of a traumatic event.

There are two claimed conditions for which independent characterization of an incident may provide a different perception of the likely severity of the event: concussion/mild TBI and PTSD. This is in part because many individuals have an inaccurate understanding of the nature, course, and outcome from concussion, and of the type of events that qualify as a traumatic stressor consistent with Diagnostic and Statistical Manual of Mental Disorders, Fifth Edition, Text Revision (DSM-5-TR; American Psychiatric Association [APA], 2022) criteria.

Characteristics of Concussion/Mild TBI

The terms concussion and mild TBI are synonymous, although concussion may be considered to be at the mild end of the range of mild TBI. Widely accepted characteristics of mild TBI are described here, with the understanding that an injury diagnosed as a concussion would be no more severe than these descriptions. The consensus diagnostic criteria for a mild TBI (Silverberg et al., 2023) include one or more of the following clinical signs: loss of consciousness immediately following the injury, alteration of mental status immediately following the injury (reduced responsiveness or inappropriate responses; slowness to respond to questions or instructions; agitated behavior; inability to follow two-part commands; or disorientation to time, place or situation); complete or partial amnesia for events immediately following the injury; or other acute neurologic signs (e.g., observed motor incoordination, seizure, or tonic posturing immediately following injury) (Silverberg et al., 2023).

A complementary but nonredundant framework for classifying mild TBI as distinct from moderate and severe TBI includes the following characteristics (Ruff et al., 2009): A mild TBI involves (1) loss of consciousness of 30 minutes or less; (2) Glasgow Coma Scale scores in the range of 13–15; (3) posttraumatic amnesia less than 24 hours; and (4) absence of skull fracture or acute intracranial abnormalities on imaging studies.

The defining characteristics of a mild TBI are important because the course and outcome from mild TBI has been examined in numerous studies, with a consistent finding that the vast majority of patients recover fully within days to no more than 3 months duration postinjury, with no statistically detectable cognitive deficits (Rohling et al., 2011, 2012). Although there has been some disagreement in the outcome literature (e.g., Pertab et al., 2009) the meta-analysis by Rohling et al. (2011) convincingly showed that no clinically meaningful or detectable cognitive deficit remained in mild TBI samples for which examinees had passed validity measures.

As such, if a review of records indicates that the examinee experienced a head injury with either no loss of consciousness, or loss of consciousness of less than 30 minutes; and Glasgow Coma Scale score of 13–15; and either no posttraumatic amnesia or duration of posttraumatic amnesia no greater than 24 hours, then the examinee would have experienced no worse than a mild TBI (assuming there were no intracranial abnormalities, such as skull fracture or intracranial bleeding). In the absence of other complicating factors, any cognitive deficits from the mild TBI would have resolved within 3 months. Accordingly, the clinician can expect that no significant cognitive deficits from a mild TBI would remain if the assessment took place more than

3 months postinjury; if impaired cognitive performance were observed, this would likely be attributable to factors other than the injury.

Characteristics of Traumatic Incidents

Some examinees during assessment will state that they have developed PTSD from a motor vehicle accident, a slip and fall accident, or other forms of injury. A recent examinee claimed to have experienced nightmares and flashbacks from a work incident in which a shelf holding boxes of printer paper bent, with three or more boxes of printer paper falling on to him from a height of approximately 18 inches above his head. For clinicians who are familiar with DSM-5-TR criteria for PTSD, this and many other claimed events would not qualify as a traumatic stressor event. From the DSM-5-TR Criterion A: "Exposure to actual or threatened death, serious injury, or sexual violence" (APA, 2022, p. 301), which is described more fully in the Diagnostic Features section that follows the PTSD criteria:

> The directly experienced traumatic events in Criterion A include, but are not limited to, exposure to war as a combatant or civilian, actual or threatened physical assault in which the threat is perceived as imminent and realistic (e.g., physical attack, robbery, mugging, childhood physical abuse), being kidnapped, being taken hostage, terrorist attack, torture, incarceration as a prisoner of war, natural or human-made disasters, and severe motor vehicle accidents. (APA, 2022, p. 305)

Note that the specifier "severe" precedes motor vehicle accidents, presumably because PTSD claims following relatively minor car accidents have proliferated. It is important to highlight that the DSM-5-TR specifies "severe" motor vehicle accidents because, despite the wide availability of the DSM-5-TR, it is all too common for a review of records to turn up a diagnosis of PTSD by a psychologist, for a nontraumatic incident such as a minor motor vehicle accident, slipping and falling without serious injury, and similar events. Responding to the degree to which the bar for incident severity has been lowered by some clinicians for diagnosing PTSD, Nancy Andreasen, one of the original authors of the diagnostic criteria for PTSD, wrote that "Giving the same diagnosis to death camp survivors and someone who has been in a motor vehicle accident diminishes the magnitude of the stressor and the significance of PTSD" (Andreasen, 2004, p. 1321).

As such, one should not simply assume that finding a diagnosis of PTSD in the records means that the examinee was carefully evaluated for PTSD and actually meets its criteria. In fact, I have reviewed several cases in which a physician or psychologist assigned a diagnosis of PTSD within a week of experiencing an incident, and in which the incident would not meet Criterion A, as a traumatic stressor. Given that the DSM-5-TR specifies a duration of more than 1 month of symptoms before PTSD can be diagnosed, the clinician assigning the diagnosis would have made an obvious error regarding duration, calling into question their familiarity with diagnostic criteria for PTSD more generally. The clever term "diagnosis momentum" has been used to describe the tendency for clinicians to repeat a diagnosis that has been assigned to a patient they are seeing, without carefully confirming that the patient actually meets criteria for the diagnosis (Croskerry, 2003). Before accepting as accurate a previously assigned diagnosis of PTSD, it is helpful to search the records for documentation that adequately documented symptoms of sufficient number and type (at least one Criterion B intrusion symptom, one Criterion C avoidance symptom, two Criterion D negative changes in cognition and mood symptoms, and two Criterion E increases in arousal symptoms), and duration (at least 1 month of symptoms). The symptoms must also be related to the incident; this is important, because some examinees may endorse sleep disturbance, which is one form of Criterion E symptoms, but records may indicate pre-incident complaints of sleep disturbance due to pain or to sleep apnea.

Establishing Background to Evaluate Consistency With Self-Report

Records may identify subtle and potentially nonintentional inaccuracies, such as an examinee who reports being an "outstanding" student but whose records indicate average high school or college grades. Records can also reveal blatant misrepresentation, such as an examinee reporting consistently excellent work performance but whose records indicate multiple firings and long periods of unemployment interspersed with periods of incarceration. Review of records prior to the assessment allows the examiner to note when such discrepancies occur and to query further, to note whether the inconsistency reflects a minor misunderstanding or suggests deliberate misrepresentation.

Selecting and Sequencing PVTs

The selection of validity measures involves balancing the competing demands of including a thorough assessment of both performance validity and symptom validity using a range of different formats, against the practical matters of time constraints and the limits of the examinee's (and perhaps the clinician's) endurance. Optimizing the amount of validity assessment in the limited amount of assessment time requires that the clinician ensures that included validity measures are normatively appropriate for the examinee, and that they involve different presentation and response formats, and that they are sequenced such that they avoid interfering with neuropsychological measures.

Assessing Performance Validity: PVTs

The validity measures should include PVTs involving different formats (e.g., oral presentation, visual presentation) and related to different kinds of cognitive processes (e.g., visual memory, verbal memory, visual search tasks). It is common practice to include one or more freestanding PVTs (Young et al., 2016), such as the TOMM, which involves visual presentation of drawings of objects to be remembered; or the WMT or MSVT, both of which involve word stimuli, also presented visually, to be remembered. Although less frequently used, the PDRT involves oral presentation of digits to be remembered, followed by visual recognition testing. The Dot Counting Test offers an alternative to memory-based PVTs, with scores based on combined accuracy and response time.

In addition, many embedded PVTs have been developed, some of which have been validated for use with many different types of patient populations. In planning an assessment, selecting embedded PVTs that have been normed with populations appropriate to the examinee allows both neuropsychological data and validity data to be gathered at the same time. Several embedded PVTs can be readily derived from tasks that would be administered in most neuropsychological assessments. For example, the Wechsler-based Digit Span tests allow for computation of reliable digit span, utilizing Digits Forward and Digits Backward (Greiffenstein et al., 1994), and the Enhanced reliable digit span measure (Reese et al., 2012) which adds performance from Digits Sequencing to the original reliable digit span measure.

Clinical Pearl

Including standard neuropsychological tests that have also been validated as embedded PVTs increases performance validity information without using extra time.

Similarly, the Recognition trial of the Rey Auditory Verbal Learning Test (Rey-AVLT) has been validated for use as an embedded PVT (Binder, 1993b), and additional embedded PVTs have also been derived from the Rey-AVLT and validated (Pliskin et al., 2021). Although a comprehensive listing of all available embedded PVTs is beyond the scope of the current book, it should be noted that many standard neuropsychological measures have had some form of an embedded PVT derived from them. However, care should be taken in using such measures to ensure that the normative sample for which recommended cutoff scores are established are consistent with the education, cultural background, age, and neurological and psychological conditions of an examinee for which the PVT is being considered. For example, computing an embedded PVT and applying cutoff scores that were developed on a simulated feigning group consisting of healthy undergraduate students would likely not be appropriate for use with an elderly examinee with 8 years of education with English as a second language; the risk of a false positive error in using such a measure could be significantly elevated.

Just as care must be taken in sequencing neuropsychological measures to ensure that stimuli from one test do not interfere with performance on another, PVTs should be sequenced in a way that avoids presenting stimuli that would potentially disrupt performance on a neighboring task. For example, the CVLT-2 manual indicates that verbal tasks should not be administered in the interval between completion of the immediate recall and delayed recall of the word list, as word stimuli from an intervening task may interfere with delayed recall and recognition of the CVLT-2 word list. Similarly, PVTs that involve word stimuli, such as the WMT and MSVT, should not be administered adjacent to a verbal memory task, such as the CVLT-2, Rey-AVLT, or the Logical Memory or Verbal Paired Associates tasks of the Wechsler Memory Scales.

PVTs that involve drawn objects should not be administered adjacent to similar neuropsychological tests to avoid contamination of one set of stimuli with the other. For example, the Boston Naming Test (Kaplan et al., 1983) should not be administered in between initial and delayed trials of the TOMM.

Assessing Self-Reported Symptom Validity: SVTs

The MMPI (in all versions) offers a particularly rich source of self-report validity through the numerous validity scales that are reported as part of standard administration. In addition to evaluating the standard validity scales provided by MMPI score reports, supplemental validity scales (e.g., the Henry-Heilbbroner Index (HHI; Henry et al., 2013) and a compositive validity index score that incorporates several MMPI validity scales in a single index (the Meyers Index; Meyers, 2002; Meyers et al., 2014) have been derived by independent researchers and may be computed by the examiner.

Given that the MMPI is primarily a broadband measure of psychological functioning, the validity scales are analogous to embedded PVTs in that they perform double duty in assessing validity while also obtaining information about psychological symptoms. For this reason, the MMPI is generally a more information-dense instrument than most alternatives, obtaining extensive psychological information while concurrently evaluating several different forms of self-report validity. As reviewed in Chapter 3, both the PAI and MCMI (all versions respectively) include validity scales; however, each has significantly fewer validity scales than the MMPI. In addition, the MMPI has a substantial research base for both its clinical scales and validity scales, all of which tend to make the MMPI a strong candidate for inclusion in an assessment battery for which the likelihood of feigned impairment is increased.

It may also be useful to include a stand-alone SVT as part of the assessment, which may be introduced at a different time point in the assessment from the MMPI, to allow for sampling of validity across the assessment process. The Structured Inventory of Malingered Symptomatology (SIMS; Widows & Smith, 2005) is a frequently used SVT, with good sensitivity and specificity for differentiating genuine from feigning patients. In addition, the SIMS has subscales that identify overreporting of different types of symptoms or problems (neurological impairment, amnestic disorders, psychosis, low intelligence, and affective disorders), allowing for detection of a range of possible overreporting approaches. With 75 True-False items and computerized online administration and scoring available, the SIMS takes approximately 15 minutes for most examinees to complete (while allowing the examiner to complete other tasks, as no examiner input is needed once the online SIMS is started).

Two symptom validity measures that are administered in a structured interview format are the Structured Interview of Reported Symptoms (SIRS; Rogers et al., 1992), and the Miller Forensic Assessment of Symptoms Test (M-FAST; Miller, 2001), both of which have been found to have good psychometric properties in differentiating overreporting groups from valid comparison groups (Detullio et al., 2019). The use of standardized measures for evaluating interview-based validity allows for greater precision in quantifying the probability that an examinee's responses should be construed as legitimate. Deciding whether to include either the SIRS or M-FAST requires weighing the potential gain in validity-related information against the amount of time required to administer each measure. The second edition of the SIRS (SIRS-2; Rogers et al., 2010) consists of more than 170 items related to feigned psychiatric symptoms and takes approximately 30–40 minutes to administer, requiring the examiner's direct involvement in reading the items and recording the examinee responses. As such, the SIRS-2 is more time-intensive than some other symptom validity measures, although it provides a wider range of areas in which the examinee may demonstrate symptom exaggeration or otherwise invalid responding.

With 25 items, and requiring only 5–10 minutes to administer, the M-FAST requires significantly less time than the SIRS-2 to administer. However, the M-FAST is characterized as a "screening" measure, and it has been recommended (Miller, 2001) that when the M-FAST indicates that an examinee is likely malingering, the clinician should administer a more comprehensive validity measure such as the SIRS-2. One option would be to administer the M-FAST routinely and administer the SIRS-2 only when M-FAST results suggest feigned psychiatric symptoms.

A final consideration as to whether to include the SIRS-2 in an assessment is whether the examinee's claim involves significant psychiatric symptoms; if so, including the SIRS-2 would allow for a more thorough assessment of validity related to psychiatric complaints. If the examinee's presentation is primarily of cognitive/neuropsychological or physical/pain complaints or deficits, then the added time necessary for the SIRS-2 may not be justified.

Focal Self-Report Measures for Differential Diagnosis

In cases involving injury-related disability claims it is common for somatization to play a role in extending the period of self-reported pain or impairment. Somatization refers to a process in which an individual becomes preoccupied and overidentified with physical symptoms that are not found to have a medical cause or that are out of proportion to any objective medical findings (Boone, 2017). Such individuals may report physical health symptoms as a result of psychological or interpersonal difficulties or stressors. Psychometrically, somatoform disorders and somatic symptom disorders have been associated with elevations on MMPI scales RC1 as well as on the brief measures Patient Health Questionnaire (PHQ-15; Kroenke et al., 2002), Modified Somatic Perception Questionnaire (MSPQ; Main, 1983), and Pain Catastrophizing Scale (PCS; Sullivan et al., 1995). At 15 items, 13 items, and 13 items respectively, the inclusion of these three self-report instruments provides additional information about the possible influence of somatization, rather than intentional feigning, aiding in making differential diagnoses.

Conducting the Assessment

This section will describe components of the assessment as they relate to evaluating the validity of an examinee's presentation. In addition, ways of seeking information that would suggest factors other than feigning are described; such information is valuable in making differential decisions between malingering, somatization, or other considerations.

Clinical Interview

The clinical interview is a standard part of nearly every psychological assessment. Although "clinical judgment" alone is not sufficiently accurate to reliably detect an invalid presentation by an examinee (e.g., Faust et al., 1988), the information provided by an examinee during the clinical interview may be compared with information from other sources. When discrepancies are noted, the examinee can be asked for clarification. For example, if an examinee denies any prior history of alcohol abuse, but records indicate previous diagnoses and inpatient treatment for alcohol dependence, the way that the examinee clarifies this discrepancy may shed light on the examinee's approach to the interview. An examinee who appears to have misinterpreted the question and accurately answered that they do not currently have an alcohol abuse problem may continue to be perceived as providing valid information, whereas an examinee who appears angry or chagrined to have had their previous alcohol use problems known may be viewed as willing to provide inaccurate information. The validity of assessment information from the latter examinee would then be regarded as potentially suspect.

Behavioral Observation

Although generally not standardized, behavioral observation can inform assessment validity when an examinee's observed behaviors and demeanor during assessment are inconsistent with behaviors in situations in which they are unaware of being observed. For example, if an examinee is observed walking briskly from their car to the clinician's office building, talking energetically on their phone, but then once in the clinic office moves slowly and apparently painfully, displaying ostensible distress, and describes being so depressed it is difficult for them to move, it would be reasonable to note the inconsistency and recalibrate estimates of the validity of the assessment data accordingly. Similarly, some examinees speak normally during initial conversational speech, but when asked to describe any problems or symptoms they have noticed following an injury, they begin stuttering while also stating that the injury has caused them to stutter at times. The emergence of stuttering following periods of normal speech suggests volitional control of the behavior and would increase the support for concluding that an examinee was feigning.

At the same time, behavioral observations offer an opportunity to seek evidence that an examinee is not feigning symptoms or impairment. This would include consistency within their behaviors and task performance across the assessment, and consistency between self-reported limitations and observed behaviors. For example, an examinee who rated their current back pain at 9 out of 10 but who sat calmly and in no apparent distress while offering this rating would suggest reduced credibility. In contrast, greater credibility would be suggested in an examinee who rated their back pain at 6/10 and who appeared to be physically uncomfortable across much of the assessment, changing positions and moving in a manner consistent with pain even when distracted by tasks or conversation.

An interesting form of inconsistency that supports a nonfeigning explanation was described in a case characterized as "neurocognitive hypochondriasis" (Boone, 2009). The patient described herself as having severe cognitive problems that had persisted 3 years after a motor vehicle accident with no loss of consciousness and no posttraumatic amnesia. As described in Boone (2009) the patient estimated that because of the injury, tasks took 6 to 10 times longer to complete, and that she had experienced a 90 % reduction in her memory, although she estimated that her memory had improved to a 10 % decline by the time of testing. She also reported a number of physical symptoms, including a persistent headache and intermittent nausea, as well as significant sleep changes. Although these self-reported deficits following the relatively mild injury would suggest the possibility of intentional feigning through self-report, the examinee's performance on neuropsychological testing was in the Above Average to Superior levels, with a full-scale IQ of 132.

In this case, there was an observed inconsistency between the examinee's self-reported problems and the examinee's actual performance on neuropsychological testing; however, this inconsistency did not suggest intentional feigning by the examinee. Rather, this was characterized by Boone (2009) as reflecting a form of somatization such as seen in the somatoform/somatic symptom disorders. Differentiating intentional feigning from nonfeigning forms of symptom overreporting will be addressed later in the chapter.

Practical Considerations During Assessment

It is standard practice to offer breaks periodically during assessments so that performance on testing is not unduly affected by fatigue. A useful practice to incorporate either at breaks or between tests is to ask the examinee whether they were able to give their best effort on the task, and whether anything interfered with their performance. Unexpected interruptions and distractions such as car alarms and cell phone notifications may occur and could disrupt encoding of a word list, or slow a processing speed task, and subjective experiences such as pain or worry may divert an examinee's attention. Documenting whether the examinee perceives that such factors interfered with their performance provides context for explaining unexpected variability in performance (e.g., a single low score on a measure of attention when other attention-related measures were within expectations). In addition, asking an examinee to confirm that they were not distracted and were able to give good effort on a PVT, when they actually failed the PVT, anticipates and eliminates distraction as a potential excuse for PVT failure.

Interpretation of Validity Measure Findings

Examining validity data from PVTs and SVTs provides information as to whether the examinee's responses on self-report measures and performance on neuropsychological tasks should be considered an actual reflection of their psychological and neurocognitive status. We will first review steps involved in evaluating self-report validity measures, followed by interpretation of PVTs.

Evaluating Self-Report Validity

Examining the results of free-standing and internal SVTs provides information about whether an examinee's self-report may be considered an accurate reflection of their status, or whether some degree of symptom overreporting is indicated in one or more domains (e.g., psychological problems, cognitive deficits, or pain/physical complaints).

This section will review self-report validity measures and the possible meanings of different degrees of elevation. Because the MMPI and PAI validity scales are reported as T-scores, the specific items and the number of items scored a particular way are not revealed by including these score ranges. However, describing score ranges for validity scales for which raw scores are used may reveal information that could be used to coach examinees in avoiding detection. As such, specific score ranges for most SVTs will not be provided, as scoring guidance will be available within the manual for any measures to be administered.

When examining broadband psychological instruments such as the MMPI, MCMI, or PAI, three aspects of protocol validity should be examined in sequence: First, did the examinee respond to a sufficient number of items to allow interpretation; second, did the examinee pay attention to the content of the items and respond in a consistent manner; third, did the examinee overreport or underreport in their responses? Because overreporting and underreporting scales on the MMPI in particular may be elevated or reduced by random responding or other forms of noncontent responding, it is important to consider whether the examinee provided responses to enough items with sufficient attention to respond consistently such that the protocol can be considered to reflect their intent.

Missing Items

For the PAI, publisher guidance (Morey, 2007) indicates that when 18 or more items remain unanswered, the examinee should be asked to complete the unanswered items, if possible. If more than 20 % of items for any given clinical subscale are unanswered, then the subscale should not be interpreted.

For the MMPI, the CNS scale consists of a count of the number of items for which no scorable response was given. This usually is due to no response being given; however, although less common than providing no response, an item is also considered nonresponsive if the examinee endorses both True and False for the same item and would also increase the CNS total score.

Note that the MMPI-2 (Butcher et al., 1989) includes 567 items, and so the validity of MMPI-2 scales is less affected by a given number of missing responses relative to the effects that the same number of missing responses would produce on the MMPI-2-RF (Ben-Porath & Tellegen, 2008) which includes 338 items, or the MMPI-3 (Ben-Porath & Tellegen, 2020), which includes 335 items.

Guidelines for both the MMPI-2-RF and MMPI-3 indicate that a CNS raw score of 1 to 14 suggests selective nonresponsiveness. Depending on which items did not receive a response, some of the scales with fewer items may be invalid due to having too few responses to adequately measure the scale. MMPI-2-RF and MMPI-3 CNS raw scores of 15 or greater indicate that scores on some scales may be invalid. CNS scores of this magnitude may occur because of difficulties with reading or comprehension, severe psychopathology, or unwillingness by the examinee to cooperate with the exam.

Recommendations for dealing with MMPI CNS raw scores either in the 1–14 range, or for 15 or above are essentially the same. Examiners should review the content of the nonresponsive items to identify any themes across the items. The effects of missing responses will depend on the specific scales to which the items contributed. MMPI-2-RF and MMPI-3 manual guidance indicates that for any scales for which fewer than 90 % of items were scorable, a lack of elevation cannot be interpreted as reflecting the absence of the problems related to the scale.

Evaluating Response Consistency

The most prominent broadband self-report instruments (MCMI, PAI, MMPI) all include one or more scales that indicate the extent to which an examinee's responses to items were consistent. Elevated scores on measures that detect inconsistency may be due to carelessness, inattentiveness, or confusion. When inconsistency scales are significantly elevated the protocol would indicate "noncontent" responding (i.e., the examinee's responses were unrelated to the meaning of the items) and so the protocol would not be interpretable. It should be noted that "failing" an inconsistency measure does not indicate feigning and should not be interpreted as an indication of symptom overreporting.

MCMI Inconsistency Scale

The MCMI-IV that indicates inconsistency is labeled the W scale (Millon et al., 2015). This scale consists of several pairs of similarly worded items; the W scale increases each time discrepant responses occur for the paired items that are similar in meaning. A significantly elevated W scale indicates that the examinee did not respond primarily to item content but may have been responding at random or carelessly; as a result, the MCMI-IV protocol cannot be interpreted.

PAI Inconsistency Scale

The PAI Inconsistency (ICN) scale reflects the number of discrepant responses given out of 10 paired responses with similar content. Publisher guidance (Morey, 2007) characterizes ICN T-scores below 64 as reflecting generally consistent responding and with adequate attention paid to item content. T-scores from 64 to 72 reflect some inconsistency in responding that could be attributable to carelessness or impression management. An ICN T-score of 73 is the average score generated by random responding, and so T-scores of 73 or above render the PAI protocol uninterpretable, as the examinee's responses would be essentially unrelated to item content (Morey, 2007).

MMPI Inconsistency Scales

Interpretive guidelines are the same for MMPI-2, MMPI-2-RF, and MMPI-3 for measures of response inconsistency, except that the MMPI-3 introduced an additional measure, Combined Response Inconsistency (CRIN), that is not present in the previous versions. Guidance for VRIN and TRIN below applies to all of these versions of the MMPI.

Variable Response Inconsistency (VRIN)

The VRIN validity scale consists of dozens of pairs of semantically similar items worded in opposite directions (True versus False to endorse the same statement). For example, if an examinee responded True to the statement "I am usually happy" and False to the statement "I am often happy", we would have no interpretable information as to examinee's happiness. Although one or two instances of semantically inconsistent responses may reflect a minor attentional lapse, each additional inconsistent response implies increasingly less valid responding to the items themselves, and the higher the number of content-inconsistent responses, the greater the departure from validity. Although the decrease in validity may be considered to be on a continuum, MMPI publisher guidance (Ben-Porath & Tellegen, 2020) is to consider protocols with VRIN T-scores of 80 or above to be invalid and noninterpretable. As such, if VRIN T-scores are 80 or above, the MMPI protocol should not be regarded as an accurate representation of the examinee's psychological status. In such cases, it may be useful to ask the examinee about what may have affected responses during testing.

Intentional random responding occurs when the examinee has the ability to respond accurately but does not do so, typically because the examinee is uncooperative. *Unintentional random responding* may occur because of an inadequate reading level, difficulty comprehending some items, inadequate familiarity with the language in which the test is administered, or reading difficulties if the examinee forgot their reading glasses and could not read the questions clearly. When the MMPI is administered with a paper response sheet, the examinee may accidentally shift their responses by one item, such that their marked response is actually intended for the item before or after the one that they marked. This would produce an essentially random responding pattern for the mismarked items, although in this case not due to examinee intent.

It should be noted that when a VRIN T-score of 80 or above invalidates the protocol, this also means that the Overreporting and Underreporting validity scales cannot be interpreted; elevations on either of these types of scales may occur because of random responding rather than intentional misrepresentation.

Clinical Pearl

If an overreporting validity scale is elevated, check to see whether VRIN or TRIN scales are elevated (T ≥ 80), to avoid inferring that symptom exaggeration, rather than random or fixed noncontent responding, has occurred.

True Response Inconsistency (TRIN)

The TRIN scale detects "fixed indiscriminant responding"; it comprises item pairs that are approximately reversed in meaning from each other, such that responding True to both (or False to both) would reflect inconsistency. TRIN becomes elevated by a tendency to respond True (or False), regardless of item content. Thus, an elevated TRIN scale can reflect either excessive True responses or excessive False responses. In both cases, TRIN T-scores of 80 or above indicate that the protocol is invalid and cannot be interpreted.

For TRIN T-scores in the 70–79 range, guidelines recommend caution in interpreting certain clinical scales. When TRIN T-scores are in this range in the True direction, RC6 and RC8 scores should be interpreted cautiously as they are less likely to accurately reflect the examinee's psychological status. For the same reason, when TRIN T-scores are in the 70–79 range in the False direction, caution is recommended in interpreting RC1 and RC2 scores.

Combined Response Inconsistency (CRIN)

In addition to VRIN and TRIN scales, the MMPI-3 introduced a new measure that combines different forms of inconsistent responding, the Combined Response Inconsistency (CRIN) scale. The CRIN scale adds the number of variable inconsistent responses, the number of inconsistent (fixed) True responses, and the number of inconsistent (fixed) False responses, for a total of 86 items pairs. This sum score indicates the overall degree of inconsistent responding within the protocol and may be elevated by examinees who intermittently respond randomly or have stretches of fixed responding (several

True or False responses without regard to item content). In such cases, CRIN may become significantly elevated even when VRIN and TRIN may not become sufficiently elevated to signal the invalid responding. CRIN T-score values from 70 to 79 indicate evidence of response inconsistency, which may be attributable to an uncooperative approach to completing the test, difficulties with reading or comprehending items, or carelessness. Although scores in this range do not necessarily invalidate the entire protocol, the different responses to similar items imply that at least some of the responses do not reflect the examinee's actual intent. Accordingly, substantive scales should be interpreted with caution for CRIN T-scores of 70–79. CRIN T-scores ≥ 80 render the protocol invalid because of excessive inconsistency.

Clinical Pearl

Before examining self-report validity scales, ensure that the examinee did not leave too many items blank and did not respond with excessive inconsistency.

Effects of Noncontent Responding on MMPI-3 Overreporting and Underreporting Validity Scales

The MMPI-3 interpretive manual describes confounds that may artifactually increase or decrease validity scale scores. Whereas nonresponding, detected by CNS (Cannot Say), tends to lower all validity scale scores, random responding, detected by VRIN (and by CRIN, for the MMPI-3), tends to increase both overreporting scales (F, Fp, Fs, FBS, and RBS) as well as underreporting scales (L and K). Fixed responding in the True direction (TRIN-T) results in artifactually elevated scores on all overreporting scales, but artifactual lowering of underreporting scales L and K. Fixed responding in the False direction (TRIN-F) results in artifactual elevation of all overreporting and underreporting scales.

Clinical Pearl

If inconsistent responding on self-report measures has been ruled, then any overreporting validity scale elevations may be presumed to have been purposeful.

Interpreting Overreporting Validity Scales

As described in Chapter 2, the MMPI, MCMI, and PAI contain both overreporting and underreporting measures. Because disability and personal injury claims primarily involve overreporting of symptoms and problems, these scales will be emphasized.

MMPI Overreporting Scales

MMPI Infrequent Responses (F)

F T-scores below 79 are interpreted as not indicating symptom overreporting. F T-scores from 80 to 89 may reflect overreporting of psychological problems, but scores in this range may result from inconsistent responding, or from significant psychopathology or emotional distress. F T-scores from 90 to 99 are also considered to reflect possible overreporting of psychological dysfunction, based on a high number of infrequent responses. VRIN and TRIN should be evaluated for inconsistent responding as a possible basis for high F scores. Although such F elevations may occur in credible individuals with significant psychopathology, symptom overreporting is considered to be a more likely explanation unless there is documented history or supporting evidence of significant psychopathology.

When F T-scores reach the range of 100 to 119, the publisher guidance indicates that "the protocol may be invalid" (Ben-Porath, 2012, p. 244). It should be noted that the F is somewhat distinct among MMPI validity scales in that even very high scores do not necessarily imply intentional symptom overreporting, as genuine, severe psychopathology may (rarely) be associated with such high F elevations. However, the items that make up the F scale are rarely endorsed, even by individuals with severe psychopathology, and the higher the F T-score values, the greater the likelihood that symptom overreporting is involved. This is especially the case when there is little or no corroborating evidence of severe psychopathology.

For an F T-score of 120, publisher guidance is that the MMPI protocol is considered invalid due to overreporting, although excessive inconsistent responding may produce such a score (Ben-Porath & Tellegen, 2020).

Clinical Pearls

Clinicians should view F T-scores as having a higher threshold for raising overreporting concerns compared with other MMPI validity scales, as high F scores may occur in individuals with genuine, severe psychopathology.

Examine VRIN-r and TRIN-r scales whenever validity scales are elevated to avoid concluding that symptom exaggeration is present when validity scale elevation may be due to inconsistent responding.

Infrequent Psychopathology Responses (Fp)

The Fp consists of a number of items that are ostensibly psychological symptoms but are actually rarely endorsed by individuals diagnosed with even severe psychopathology. Because of this, the Fp is less likely to be elevated by emotional distress or psychopathology than the F scales, allowing for improved detection of feigned psychopathology. Assuming that inconsistent responding has been considered, Fp T-scores of 70–79 suggest possible overreporting of psychological symptoms, although severe psychopathology may account for scores in this range. Fp scores of 80–99 reflect endorsement of a significant number of items rarely endorsed by those with severe psychopathology, with higher scores indicating a greater likelihood of overreporting as opposed to genuine psychopathology. If inconsistent responding has been considered and ruled out, Fp scores ≥100 render the protocol invalid because of symptom overreporting.

Infrequent Somatic Responses (Fs)

The Fs includes 16 items related to somatic symptoms that are infrequently endorsed by medical patients undergoing treatment for a range of medical conditions. Fs is intended to detect overreporting of somatic symptoms. Fs scores below 80 are not interpreted as reflecting overreporting of somatic symptoms. Fs scores 80–99 may be due to inconsistent responding or to overreporting of somatic symptoms but also may reflect the experience of genuine medical conditions if the medical condition is significant or if the individual has several medical conditions. Fs scores ≥100 may be invalid; however, publisher guidance does not indicate that such scores necessarily invalidate the MMPI-3 protocol (Ben-Porath & Tellegen, 2020). This is likely due to findings that the endorsement of the 16 items in the Fs by genuine medical patients is not as uncommon as for the items that comprise the F and Fp scales (Wygant et al., 2009). As such, inferences about somatic symptom overreporting when Fs is elevated should be made cautiously, and with consideration of objective findings regarding the medical severity or complexity of the examinee.

Fake Bad Scale (FBS)

The FBS was initially developed for the MMPI-2 by Lees-Haley et al. (1991), who identified a number of somewhat disparate items that he found to differentiate individuals responding genuinely from those identified as feigning disability. The MMPI manual describes FBS elevations as reflecting "an unusual combination of responses that is associated with noncredible reporting of somatic and/or cognitive symptoms".

For FBS T-scores below 78, no overreporting is indicated. For T-scores 78–89, possible overreporting of somatic and/or cognitive symptoms is indicated, although the possibility of inconsistent responding as the reason for this elevation should be considered by examining consistency measures. T-scores ≥90 indicate overreporting of somatic and/or cognitive symptoms, and the protocol may be invalid.

Response Bias Scale (RBS)

The RBS was developed based on empirical association with failure on PVTs. RBS T-scores below 75 do not indicate overreporting. T-scores in the 75–89 range indicate possibility overreporting associated with noncredible memory complaints, while T-scores ≥90 are strongly associated with noncredible memory complaints.

MMPI Composite Validity Index

Meyers Index

In addition to examining individual MMPI validity scales, a composite validity measure, developed by John Meyers, assigns points (0, 1, or 2) for several MMPI validity scales. The sum of these points is the Meyers Index (Meyers et al., 2014), which reflects a composite measure of the overall degree of exaggeration or overreporting on the MMPI. The original Meyers Index was created for the MMPI-2 (Meyers, 2002) and was subsequently adapted for the MMPI-2-RF (Meyers et al., 2014). Table 2 presents the T-score ranges for computing the Meyers Index for the MMPI-2 and MMPI-2-RF. Although cutoff scores for many validity measures are not provided in this book to maintain test security, the T-scores for validity scales are derived and cannot readily be estimated from raw scores; in addition, the mapping of individual item content to different validity scales is not readily available to examinees.

The weights (i.e., values of 1 or 2) assigned to each validity scale are simply added up to create the composite Meyers Index. If the examinee scores are outside the ranges listed, they are not assigned a weight and would have a Meyers Index value of zero. As an example, suppose an examinee's MMPI-2-RF scores were F-r=98; Fp-r=65; Fs=85; FBS-r=95; RBS=101. Referring to Table [MI-r] we can see that F-r T-score of 98 is ≥90 and so would receive a weighted score of 2. The Fp-r T-score of 65 would be weighted as zero because it is below the 75–89 range; it does not increase the Meyers Index – Revised score. The Fs T-score of 85 is in the 75–89 range and so would receive a weighted score of 1. The FBS-r T-score of 95 is greater than 90 and so receives a weighted score of 2, and the RBS T-score of 101 is also greater than 90 and also receives a weighted score of 2.

To compute the Meyers Index – Revised score, we would have 2 points from F-r, 0 points from Fp-r, 1 point from Fs, 2 points from FBS-r, and 2 points from RBS: 2+0+1+2+2=7. The Meyers Index – Revised score of 7 would then be compared with classification accuracy data published by previous researchers. Scores of ≥5 on the Meyers Index – Revised have been found to be highly specific to samples identified as malingering or instructed to feign impairment, with a specificity of .96 reported by Meyers et al. (2014). As a reminder, specificity of .96 means that only .04 (4%) of a nonmalingering/nonfeigning sample would earn a score of ≥5 on the Meyers Index – Revised.

Table 2. Weightings of scores on validity scales for the original (MI) and revised (MI-r) Meyers Index

	MMPI-2 scales for MI				MMPI-2-RF scales for MI-r				
Scale	**Scores**	**Weight**	**Scores**	**Weight**	**Scale**	**Scores**	**Weight**	**Scores**	**Weight**
F-K (raw)	1–9	1	>10	2	F-r	75–89	1	>90	2
FBS (raw)	25–29	1	>30	2	Fp-r	75–89	1	>90	2
O-S (raw)	100–149	1	>150	2	Fs	75–89	1	>90	2
F	75–89	1	>90	2	FBS-r	75–89	1	>90	2
F(p)	75–89	1	>90	2	RBS	75–89	1	>90	2
Ds-r	75–89	1	>90	2					
ES	21–30	1	<20	2					

Note. All scores are T-scores unless otherwise noted. F-K = F-K raw score; FBS = Fake Bad Scale (raw score); F(p) = Infrequency-Psychopathology scale Ds-r = Dissimulation Scale-revised ES = Ego-Strength; O-S = Obvious – Subtle. F-r = Infrequent Responses; Fp-r = Infrequent Psychopathology Responses; Fs = Infrequent Somatic Responses; FBS-r = Symptom Validity (previously Fake Bad Scale); RBS = Response Bias Scale.

Both the original Meyers Index (MI) for the MMPI-2 and the Meyers Index for the MMPI-2-RF (MI-r) have demonstrated good classification accuracy in distinguishing known feigning or malingering samples from genuine responders. In one study, only 2% of nonmalingering chronic pain patients produced a MI score of 5 or above (98% specificity), whereas 63% of a sample identified as definite MPRD had an MI or 5 or above (63% sensitivity) (Bianchini et al., 2008). In a similar study in which patients had mild or moderate-severe TBI, a MI score of 5 or above occurred in only 5% of the sample (95% specificity), while 52% of those identified as likely malingering (MND) scored 5 or above (Greve et al., 2006). The MI-r has shown similar classification accuracy characteristics for the MMPI-2-RF. As of this writing, the MI has not been updated for use with the MMPI-3; however, because all validity scales from the MMPI-2-RF that contributed to the Meyers Index are also available on the MMPI-3, and are also reported as T-scores, it is very likely the Meyers Index can be computed and interpreted for the MMPI-3 the same as for the MMPI-2-RF.

MCMI Overreporting Scales

The MCMI Debasement (Z) scale (Millon et al., 2015) is intended to detect overreporting and self-deprecation, and elevated scores on this scale may serve as an indication of invalid presentation. However, research on the MCMI validity scales has raised concerns about relatively weak classification accuracy, and separate research groups have recommended that the MCMI validity scales not be utilized as in any substantial way to evaluate symptom validity without further empirical support (Sellbom & Bagby, 2008; Wygant et al., 2019). As such, it is recommended that MCMI overreporting scales, if used, not be assigned significant weight in interpreting assessment validity.

PAI Overreporting Scales

Negative Impression Management (NIM)

The NIM (Morey, 2007) indicates endorsement of unrealistically severe symptoms or problems, although publisher guidelines caution that the NIM is not intended specifically as a malingering scale. T-scores below 73 on the NIM indicate no significant negative distortion in the examinee's presentation, while moderate elevations (T-scores 73 to 83) indicate a degree of exaggeration of complaints and problems. T-scores 84 to 91 are associated with a greater likelihood of exaggeration, while T-scores at or above 92 are associated with either careless responding, extremely negative self-presentation, or malingering (Morey, 2007).

Malingering Index (MAL)

The MAL (Morey, 2007) reflects a pattern of item endorsement that has been associated with overreporting and unlikely to occur in honest responders. T-scores of 84 or above suggest possible malingering, while T-scores of 111 or above are very unusual among genuine clinical samples and instead are associated almost exclusively with feigning of severe psychopathology.

Miller Forensic Assessment of Symptoms Test (M-FAST)

As noted previously, the M-FAST (Miller, 2001) is considered to be a screening measure for validity concerns and so should not serve as the sole source of self-report validity data. In addition, the M-FAST detects indications of feigned psychopathology but does not adequately detect feigned cognitive symptoms. As such, if an examinee were to pass the M-FAST the clinician could be more confident that the examinee was not feigning psychopathology; however, passing the M-FAST would not indicate whether or not the examinee was feigning cognitive symptoms. Guidance on interpreting M-FAST scores may be found in the manual.

If an examinee scores in a manner consistent with symptom exaggeration on the M-FAST, the clinician should interpret this as added evidence to the possibility that the examinee is feigning, but the clinician should seek additional information that may further support or disconfirm the hypothesis. This may include administering the SIRS or examining validity scales from the MMPI or other broadband measure, keeping in mind that no single validity score should be relied upon to conclude that an examinee is or is not feigning.

Structured Inventory of Malingered Symptomatology (SIMS)

Elevations on any of the five subscales in the SIMS (Widows & Smith, 2005), namely psychosis, neurological impairment, amnestic disorders, low intelligence, and affective disorders, can indicate whether the examinee appears to be overreporting one or more specific types of conditions, and the SIMS total score serves as an index of the overall degree of overreporting. However, the SIMS has much less of a research base than the MMPI, much of which is based on simulator studies rather than clinical samples. As such, ostensible failing scores on SIMS subscale or total scores should be assigned less weight in decisions about validity than scales with a strong research base, such as the MMPI. Consult the SIMS manual for guidance on specific score interpretation.

Structured Inventory of Reports Symptoms (SIRS-2)

Described by some as the "gold standard" for detecting feigned or exaggerated psychopathology (Wygant et al., 2019), the SIRS-2 (Rogers et al., 2010) can serve as a significant source of evidence concerning the presence or absence of malingering of psychological disorders. While the SIRS-2 manual should be consulted for specific scoring guidance, clinicians who administer the SIRS-2 can place significant weight on the results of this measure in reaching conclusions about the presence or absence of feigned or exaggerated psychopathology. However, as with the M-FAST, results of the SIRS-2 do not likely have sufficient evidence for use in detecting feigned cognitive symptoms.

Evaluating Performance Validity

Performance validity may be viewed as being on a continuum, with optimal effort and focus on tasks being at one extreme, lower or variable effort in the mid-range, and intentionally failing on tasks at the other extreme. In assessments related to disability and personal injury, a general underlying question to be addressed is whether the claimant is experiencing a condition or deficit that is attributable to the injury, and if so, what is the severity of the condition or deficit. To this end, the assessment of performance validity is directed towards determining whether ostensible deficits on neuropsychological or other performance-based tasks may be attributable to invalid effort rather than to the injury.

In order to address this question, the clinician must consider not only individual PVT results in isolation but must consider the overall pattern of PVT scores in light of the examinee's demographic characteristics, established or suspected neurological, medical, or psychological conditions, and the classification accuracy characteristics of each PVT at the obtained score.

With this in mind, the current section will involve a discussion of interpretive considerations for PVT measures in general. One of the most important considerations is whether the PVT has been validated for use with individuals similar to the examinee. Specifically, has the PVT been administered to individuals within the same age range, level of education, and any potentially significant neurological or psychological conditions. As noted frequently, patients with Alzheimer's dementia in particular, but also other forms of significant neuropathology such as cerebrovascular accident, severe TBI, other forms of dementia, as well as intellectual disability or schizophrenia, may perform significantly below cutoffs established on samples with less severe pathology. It is very important to know whether any conditions or background factors associated with the examinee may be associated with an increased risk of false positive errors. Referring to the user manual for standalone PVTs, or the published research literature for embedded PVTs, can help to establish whether use of the PVT is appropriate.

Interpreting most PVT scores involves noting how close to cutoff scores the examinee has scored. In borderline cases, where the examinee's score is just slightly beyond the cutoff score, the chances that the score is due more to nonfeigning factors such as a lapse in attention or other distraction is higher. On the other hand, the farther an examinee's scores are beyond the cutoff score, the greater the confidence one can have that the results reflect invalid effort (either intentional underperformance or lack of cooperation with testing).

> **Clinical Pearl**
>
> PVTs do not have a static sensitivity or specificity value but have different sensitivity and specificity values at different scores and for different conditions.

Summary of Steps for Interpreting Validity Measure Results

The numbered list below may serve as a checklist for evaluating the self-reported symptom validity and performance validity measures. The specific measures used will depend on the instruments used, but each of these issues should be considered based on the available assessment data.

1. Did the examinee respond to a sufficient number of self-report items to produce an interpretable profile? Check the MMPI Cannot Say (CNS) scale or visually inspect other measures.
2. Did the examinee understand and respond in a consistent way to items and questions? Examine self-report consistency or noncontent responding scales such as the CRIN, VRIN, and TRIN scales of the MMPI; W inconsistency scale of the MCMI; and ICN Inconsistency scale of the PAI. These first two checks allow us to know whether or not the examinee's pattern of responding reflects intentional engagement with the items.
3. Examine SVT scales for overreporting or underreporting. If overreporting is suggested (e.g., MMPI F scales), take notice of (a) the degree of overreporting or underreporting (e.g., T of 80 vs. T of 120); and (b) the number of validity scale elevations (one scale, or multiple scales). If limited to a

single validity scale elevation, some of the rest of the self-report data may be accurate, but accuracy declines in proportion to the number of elevated validity scales. (c) Consider whether the symptom validity scale elevations reflect endorsement primarily of unusual, bizarre, infrequent items (F) or whether they are limited to one domain, such as somatic complaints (Fs), in which case consider whether the elevation reflects misunderstanding of some physical/somatic terms. This can be clarified with the patient if MMPI endorsed items are indicated.

4. Consider alternative explanations for elevated overreporting scales, including (to some extent) somatization, psychosis, or severe distress. Consider information from clinical interview, records, and different self-report measures, to examine whether a consistent, coherent pattern appears to be expressed (e.g., consistent overreporting of physical/somatic symptoms as a function of somatization). If there are inconsistencies over time or across self-report measures, intentional misrepresentation through symptom exaggeration becomes more likely than somatization alone.
5. Examine any stand-alone SVTs (e.g., SIMS). Consider whether any of the examinee's demographic characteristics or conditions (medical, psychological, neuropsychological) would explain apparent SVT failures.
6. Examine standalone performance validity measure scores (e.g., TOMM, WMT, MSVT) taking into account the degree to which the measure has been adequately validated for use with examinees of similar demographic and diagnostic backgrounds. Take note of whether a significant neurological condition such as Alzheimer's dementia may be present that could confound interpretation of the PVT (i.e., if the PVT is affected by Alzheimer's or other significant conditions).
7. Examine embedded PVTs (e.g., Reliable Digit Span), taking into account the degree to which it has been adequately validated for use with examinees of similar demographic and diagnostic backgrounds, and whether neurological conditions are present that could affect PVT performance.
8. Note whether any validity measure failures appeared to have been isolated incidents and note when during the assessment they occurred. If due to a temporary drop in cooperation, interruption of testing, or similar brief alterations, consider whether neuropsychological test data obtained near the same time may have been similarly affected by disruption.

Integrating Assessment Data

Once assessment data have been gathered and scored, these results should be reviewed and integrated with data from record review, clinical interview, and any collateral information. For purposes of assessing validity, the primary questions to address are whether information from self-report is valid and can be used to make inferences about psychological functioning; and whether performance on neuropsychological and other performance-based tasks is valid and can be used to make inferences about possible impairment.

The MND and MPRD malingering criteria provide useful conceptual frameworks for integrating this information. Although it is not necessary to formally assign or exclude a malingering diagnosis, both the MND and MPRD utilize the following valuable principles: 1. Consider information from multiple sources, noting discrepancies and inconsistencies; 2. Use well-validated SVT and PVTs that are appropriate for the examinee characteristics; 3. Do not rely on any single validity score to conclude that an examinee has malingered or otherwise misrepresented themselves (a possible exception to this would be below-chance failure of a forced-choice PVT, although even this finding would require consideration of possible alternative explanations); 4. Conceptualize evidence of feigning in probabilistic terms (i.e., possible, probable, or definite malingering), recognizing that some assessments may involve variable effort and that the psychometric properties of validity measures includes a certain percentage of false-positive errors. Finally, both MND and MPRD guidelines require considering factors other than intentional feigning that may explain apparent overreporting of symptoms or failure on PVTs. The next section reviews such factors.

Differentiating Malingering From Nonmalingering Factors

Some patients report ongoing cognitive problems and symptoms after a relatively benign concussion or subconcussive head injury and as a result may remain off work or under medical care for weeks or months. However, referral for neuropsychological assessment finds that their cognitive performance is entirely normal, and they pass all, or nearly all, performance validity measures. These patients appear to believe that they have persistent, significant concussion-related symptoms, even when objective testing determines that they do not; they describe themselves as impaired, but performance validity measures indicate that they are giving good effort on testing. A number of psychosocial factors have been identified that likely contribute to this phenomenon.

Postconcussion Syndrome

Subjective complaints are common following concussion, such as headache, light sensitivity, dizziness, concentration and memory complaints, irritability, and sleep disturbance. While these complaints resolve within weeks for the majority of patients, some report persistent symptoms for months or even years after a concussion. The term "postconcussion syndrome" has been used to refer to persistence of these subjective symptoms beyond 3 months after a concussion (e.g., Mittenberg & Strauman, 2000). Although diagnostic criteria for Postconcussion syndrome were previously established in the International Classification of Diseases, 10th Revision (ICD-10; World Health Organization [WHO], 2016) and proposed in the Diagnostic and Statistical Manual of Mental Disorders, Fourth Edition (DSM-IV; APA, 1994) this diagnosis was not added to subsequent editions of the DSM. A number of researchers have found that ostensible Postconcussion syndrome symptoms are better explained by psychological factors such as emotional disturbance or chronic pain (e.g., Belanger et al., 2005; Ponsford et al., 2012; Iverson & McCracken, 1997), or by involvement in disability claims (e.g., Binder & Rohling, 1996).

However, an important factor that likely contributes to Postconcussion syndrome is that these patients tend to underestimate how frequently symptoms that are often associated with concussion (e.g., headache, fatigue, cognitive errors) actually occur in individuals without a history of concussion (e.g., Ferguson et al., 1999; Gouvier et al., 1992). Because of this they are likely to misattribute these common experiences to the concussion rather than recognizing them as an ordinary experience. Several related terms ("diagnosis threat", "expectation as etiology", and "good old days bias"), described below, have been used to describe patients who are not feigning impairment but who inaccurately believe they have developed cognitive problems from an injury.

Diagnosis threat (Suhr & Gunstad, 2002) refers to activation of negative expectations when attention is directed to having experienced a mild TBI (Suhr & Gunstad, 2002, 2005). Several studies have shown that subjective self-reported cognitive symptoms are higher when a personal history of mild TBI is made explicit, activating diagnosis threat and the associated characteristics of memory and concentration deficits, or other symptoms such as dizziness, headaches, and light sensitivity (Carter-Allison et al., 2016).

However, it appears that the effects of diagnosis threat are limited to subjective cognitive complaints and do not typically affect actual cognitive performance to a significant degree (Ozen & Fernandes, 2010).

Expectation as etiology (Mittenberg et al., 1992) refers to the potential effects on a patient's subjective perception of having persistent symptoms or deficits following concussion that may actually reflect ordinary experiences that receive increased attention following the concussion, and that are misattributed to the concussion. Many people with no history of concussion have similar expectations for the kinds of symptoms they might experience after a concussion. As such, after experiencing a concussion, some patients will be on the lookout for signs of these expected symptoms and then attribute them to the concussion. However, it has been found that many ostensible "post-concussion" symptoms are in fact commonly experienced by healthy individuals with no history of concussion. The ordinary forgetfulness and lapses in concentration that happen regularly to nonconcussed individuals may, following concussion, receive increased attention by the patient and be interpreted as a newly acquired symptom or deficit caused by the concussion. This phenomenon overlaps somewhat with the "good old days bias" (Gunstad & Suhr, 2001).

The "good old days" bias refers to the finding that some individuals with persistent cognitive complaints following concussion tend to overestimate pre-injury functioning and underestimate pre-injury symptoms and problems. A concussion or other injury becomes a "landmark" by which one's current symptoms or problems represent a negative change from an ostensibly better previous state. The perception of one's current state as being worse than before the concussion is heightened by the phenomenon of inflating one's pre-concussion functioning, hence the term "good old days" bias.

These factors may lead an examinee to inaccurately self-report that they are experiencing significant symptoms and deficits, which may appear to reflect intentional disability exaggeration. However, when an examinee provides elevated self-reported subjective cognitive complaints but performs within expectations on actual cognitive testing, this suggests that the elevated self-report complaints are likely due to the operation of "diagnosis threat", "good old days bias", or similar processes that lead them to focus attention on and amplify normal cognitive errors and to underestimate the frequency of such normal experiences prior to the injury. This misattribution of ordinary cognitive errors and somatic sensations to a specific injury such as concussion would generally not involve intentional or conscious exaggeration, as in malingering, but would reflect nonconscious symptom exaggeration. This phenomenon is similar to, and likely overlaps with, somatization, which refers primarily to excessive physical complaints. However, the term "cognitive hypochondriasis" has been proposed by Kyle Boone to refer to somatization-like processes when the emphasis is primarily on cognitive complaints (Boone, 2009).

Somatization

An important differential diagnostic consideration is between somatization and either MND or MPRD. The criteria for each of these was described earlier. In this section, we review features of somatization and how it is distinct from both MND and MPRD.

Somatization occurs when an individual becomes preoccupied with physical symptoms that either are not found to have a medical cause or that are out of proportion to any objective medical findings, and the person may be "overidentified" with their symptoms (Boone, 2017). Those who have elevated somatization tend to report physical health symptoms as a result of psychological or interpersonal difficulties or stressors.

Somatization is conceptualized as involving nonconscious exaggeration of symptoms, whereas malingering involves conscious and intentional exaggeration. In other words, although somatization involves overreporting of symptoms, the individual is not aware that they are engaging in exaggeration. Instead, factors including attentional bias toward physical sensations, a tendency to interpret various somatic or cognitive experiences as reflecting pathology, and to become more distressed and preoccupied by them in a positive feedback loop, are believed to contribute to somatization.

Although the DSM-5-TR diagnostic category most closely associated with somatization is somatic symptom disorders (previously termed somatoform disorders in the DSM-IV), not all cases involving elevated somatization will necessarily meet DSM criteria for a somatic symptom disorder, and so the DSM criteria alone will not necessarily differentiate somatization from MND or MPRD. That is, an examinee could be experiencing somatization that results in elevations on certain validity scales but may not meet full DSM criteria for a somatic symptom disorder. However, there are a number of findings from psychometric test data and from record reviews that help to distinguish somatization from MND or MPRD.

Other Factors That May Produce False Positive Findings

As has been noted previously, PVTs are not perfect measures of performance validity. Even though they are calibrated to minimize false positive errors and to detect only performance involving poor effort, there are a number of factors that can contribute to PVT failure in individuals who are not attempting to feign impairment. Perhaps the most notable of these is Alzheimer's dementia, which has been found repeatedly to result in "failing" performance on memory-based PVTs including the TOMM, WMT, and MSVT, as well as embedded PVTs such as the Rey-AVLT Recognition test.

However, other neurological conditions, and more severe psychiatric conditions such as schizophrenia have been associated with reduced performance on PVTs, such that the risk of false positive errors increases if standard cutoff scores are used with such instruments. This emphasizes the importance not only of seeking information about an examinee prior to and during the assessment to determine whether conditions may be present that would affect PVT interpretation. In addition, this highlights the importance of developing familiarity with the research literature on PVT performance, such that findings that link certain conditions to reduced specificity for a PVT can be identified.

Drawing Conclusions

Once data have been reviewed and the clinician has determined whether assessment results are valid, partially valid, or invalid due to excessive feigning of symptoms or deficits, the assessment report can include statements that address the validity findings. If there are no validity concerns then the report can simply include a statement that the examinee appears to have responded in a forthright manner (i.e., SVT scales were valid) and appeared to give adequate effort during assessment tasks (i.e., PVT measures indicated valid effort).

However, when one or more SVT scales indicate overreporting, the report should include a statement to this effect. The statement should reflect the degree and scope of SVT elevations; for example, a single elevation on the MMPI F scale, with no other SVT elevations, would merit a brief statement that the examinee may have overreported symptoms, but without invalidating the MMPI protocol or raising significant concerns about self-report. However, in cases in which multiple MMPI validity scales are significantly elevated, the report should likely include a statement indicating that, because of significant symptom exaggeration, the MMPI protocol was invalidated and clinical scales could not be interpreted. Furthermore, the report should include a cautionary statement that because of evidence of misrepresentation in the form of significant symptom exaggeration, the examinee's self-reported symptoms and complaints should be interpreted with caution, and objective findings rather than the examinee's self-report should be given weight in making decisions about any impairment or need for treatment.

Similar guidance applies to evaluating performance validity; if all PVT measures are passed then a statement indicating that the examinee appeared to give good effort during testing may be included. It is fairly common for one PVT to be "failed" in the sense of being below empirical cutoffs, and the more PVTs administered, the greater the likelihood of a single PVT being failed despite the intention of the examinee to provide good effort. As such, failing a single PVT, particularly if the score was near the cutoff, should not likely warrant significant validity concerns.

However, the more PVTs that are failed, and the further the scores are from recommended cutoff scores, the greater the evidence of invalid effort. Statements should reflect the graded nature of the evidence of PVT failure; evidence of a moderate degree of PVT failure would warrant a statement that the results of testing likely do not reflect the examinee's true capacity, as incomplete effort appeared to have been given during some portions of the assessment. Conversely, failing numerous PVTs and to a significant degree would warrant a statement that the results of testing were invalid due to intentional feigning of disability, whether or not a formal diagnosis of malingering (i.e., MND or MPRD) is assigned. For assessments in which an examinee's performance is clearly invalid, and when injury characteristics are known to have been relatively benign (e.g., minor head injury without alteration of consciousness or posttraumatic amnesia or abnormal Glasgow Coma Scale scores), one can conclude with the simple statement that "the assessment provides no valid evidence of impairment attributable to the incident".

Book Summary

This book was intended to describe the utility of symptom and performance validity measures in assessment, as well as the conceptual underpinnings and empirical support for the use of such measures. Clinicians who may be new to validity measures are encouraged to carefully review specific validity measures they may be considering to ensure that they are appropriate for intended examinees. Becoming familiar with published malingering diagnostic systems (Slick et al., 1999, and Bianchini et al., 2005) will provide a framework for more clearly differentiating patients presenting with genuine disability from patients engaging in disability exaggeration. Although this book was intended to provide useful guidance on many of the most frequently used symptom validity measures and performance validity measures, many researchers are actively involved in developing and refining validity measures, and it is recommended that clinicians regularly consult the research literature for new developments in the assessment of symptom and performance validity.

References

Alverson, W.A., O'Rourke, J.J.F., & Soble, J.R. (2019). The Word Memory Test genuine memory impairment profile discriminates genuine memory impairment from invalid performance in a mixed clinical sample with cognitive impairment. *The Clinical Neuropsychologist, 33*(8), 1420–1435. https://doi.org/10.1080/13854046.2019.1599071

Alwes, Y.R., Clark, J.A., Berry, D.T.R., & Granacher, R.P. (2008). Screening for feigning in a civil forensic setting. *Journal of Clinical and Experimental Neuropsychology, 30*(2), 133–140. https://doi.org/10.1080/13803390701260363

American Psychiatric Association. (1994). *Diagnostic and Statistical Manual of Mental Disorders* (4th ed.). American Psychiatric Association.

American Psychiatric Association. (2022). *Diagnostic and Statistical Manual of Mental Disorders* (5th ed., Text Revision). American Psychiatric Association. https://doi.org/10.1176/appi.books.9780890425787

Andreasen, N.C. (2004). Acute and delayed posttraumatic stress disorders: A history and some issues. *American Journal of Psychiatry, 161*(8), 1321–1323. https://doi.org/10.1176/appi.ajp.161.8.1321

Bayen, E., Ruet, A., Jourdan, C., Ghout, I., Meaude, L., Pradat-Diehl, P., Nelson, G., Vallat-Azouvi, C., Charanton, J., Aegerter, P., & Azouvi, P. (2019). Lawsuit and traumatic brain injury: The relationship between long-lasting sequelae and financial compensation in litigants. Results from the PariS-TBI study. *Frontiers in Neurology, 10*, Article 320. https://doi.org/10.3389/fneur.2019.00320

Belanger, H.G., Curtiss, G., Demery, J.A., Lebowitz, B.K., & Vanderploeg, R.D. (2005). Factors moderating neuropsychological outcomes following mild traumatic brain injury: A meta-analysis. *Journal of the International Neuropsychological Society : JINS, 11*(3), 215–227. https://doi.org/10.1017/S1355617705050277

Ben-Porath, Y.S. (2012). *Interpreting the MMPI-2-RF*. University of Minnesota Press.

Ben-Porath, Y.S., & Sellbom, M. (2023). *Interpreting the MMPI-3*. University of Minnesota Press.

Ben-Porath, Y.S., & Tellegen, A. (2008). *MMPI–2–RF: Manual for Administration, Scoring and Interpretation*. University of Minnesota Press.

Ben-Porath, Y.S., & Tellegen, A. (2020). *Minnesota Multiphasic Personality Inventory-3 (MMPI-3): Manual for administration, scoring, and interpretation*. Pearson.

Bianchini, K.J., Curtis, K.L., & Greve, K.W. (2006). Compensation and malingering in traumatic brain injury: A dose-response relationship? *The Clinical Neuropsychologist, 20*(4), 831–847. https://doi.org/10.1080/13854040600875203

Bianchini, K.J., Etherton, J.L., Greve, K.W., Heinly, M.T., & Meyers, J.E. (2008). Classification accuracy of MMPI-2 validity scales in the detection of pain-related malingering: A known-groups study. *Assessment, 15*(4), 435–449. https://doi.org/10.1177/1073191108317341

Bianchini, K.J., Greve, K.W., & Glynn, G. (2005). On the diagnosis of malingered pain-related disability: Lessons from cognitive malingering research. *The Spine Journal, 5*(4), 404–417. https://doi.org/10.1016/j.spinee.2004.11.016

Binder L. M. (1993a). Assessment of malingering after mild head trauma with the Portland Digit Recognition Test. *Journal of Clinical and Experimental Neuropsychology, 15*(2), 170–182. https://doi.org/10.1080/01688639308402555

Binder, L. (1993b). The Rey AVLT recognition memory task measures motivational impairment after mild head trauma. *Archives of Clinical Neuropsychology, 8*(2), 137–147. https://doi.org/10.1016/0887-6177(93)90031-U

Binder, L. M., Larrabee, G. J., & Millis, S. R. (2014). Intent to fail: Significance testing of forced choice test results. *The Clinical Neuropsychologist, 28*(8), 1366–1375. https://doi.org/10.1080/13854046.2014.978383

Binder, L. M., & Rohling, M. L. (1996). Money matters: A meta-analytic review of the effects of financial incentives on recovery after closed-head injury. *The American Journal of Psychiatry, 153*(1), 7–10. https://doi.org/10.1176/ajp.153.1.7

Boone, K. B. (2009). Fixed belief in cognitive dysfunction despite normal neuropsychological scores: neurocognitive hypochondriasis? *The Clinical Neuropsychologist, 23*(6), 1016–1036. https://doi.org/10.1080/13854040802441135

Boone, K. B. (2017). Self-deception in somatoform conditions: Differentiating between conscious and nonconscious symptom feigning. In K. B. Boone (Ed.), *Neuropsychological evaluation of somatoform and other functional somatic conditions: Assessment primer* (pp. 3–42). Routledge/Taylor & Francis Group. https://doi.org/10.4324/9781315266992-1

Boone, K. B., Lu, P., & Herzberg, D. S. (2002). *The Dot Counting Test.* Western Psychological Services.

Boone, K. B., Salazar, X., Lu, P., Warner-Chacon, K., & Razani, J. (2002). The Rey 15-Item Recognition Trial: A technique to enhance sensitivity of the rey 15-item memorization Test. *Journal of Clinical and Experimental Neuropsychology, 24*(5), 561–573. https://doi.org/10.1076/jcen.24.5.561.1004

Burton, V., Vilar-Lopez, R., & Puente, A. E. (2012). Measuring effort in neuropsychological evaluations of forensic cases of Spanish speakers. *Archives of Clinical Neuropsychology, 27*(3), 262–267. https://doi.org/10.1093/arclin/acs026

Butcher, J. N., Arbisi, P. A., Atlis, M. M., & McNulty, J. L. (2003). The construct validity of the Lees-Haley Fake Bad Scale. Does this scale measure somatic malingering and feigned emotional distress? *Archives of Clinical Neuropsychology, 18*(5), 473–485.

Butcher, J. N., Dahlstrom, W. G., Graham, J. R., Tellegen, A. & Kaemmer, B. (1989). *Minnesota Multiphasic Personality Inventory-2 (MMPI-2): Manual for administration and scoring.* University of Minnesota Press.

Carter-Allison, S. N., Potter, S., & Rimes, K. (2016). Diagnosis threat and injury beliefs after mild traumatic brain injury. *Archives of Clinical Neuropsychology, 31*(7), 727–737. https://doi.org/10.1093/arclin/acw062

Chafetz, M., & Underhill, J. (2013). Estimated costs of malingered disability. *Archives of Clinical Neuropsychology, 28*(7), 633–639. https://doi.org/10.1093/arclin/act038

Clark, L. R., Stricker, N. H., Libon, D. J., Delano-Wood, L., Salmon, D. P., Delis, D. C., & Bondi, M. W. (2012). Yes/No versus forced-choice recognition memory in mild cognitive impairment and Alzheimer's disease: patterns of impairment and associations with dementia severity. *The Clinical Neuropsychologist, 26*(7), 1201–1216. https://doi.org/10.1080/13854046.2012.728626

Constantinou, M., & McCaffrey, R. J. (2003). Using the TOMM for evaluating children's effort to perform optimally on neuropsychological measures. *Child Neuropsychology, 9*(2), 81–90. https://doi.org/10.1076/chin.9.2.81.14505

Crișan, I., & Sava, F.A. (2025). Validity assessment in Eastern Europe: Cross-validation of the Dot Counting Test and MODEMM against the TOMM-1 and Rey-15 in a Romanian mixed clinical sample. *Archives of Clinical Neuropsychology, 40*(3), 614–625. https://doi.org/10.1093/arclin/acad085

Croskerry, P. (2003). The importance of cognitive errors in diagnosis and strategies to minimize them. *Academic Medicine, 78*(8), 775–780. https://doi.org/10.1097/00001888-200308000-00003

Dean, A.C., Victor, T.L., Boone, K.B., & Arnold, G. (2008). The relationship of IQ to effort test performance. *The Clinical Neuropsychologist, 22*(4), 705–722. https://doi.org/10.1080/13854040701440493

Dean, A.C., Victor, T.L., Boone, K.B., Philpott, L.M., & Hess, R.A. (2009). Dementia and effort test performance. *The Clinical Neuropsychologist, 23*(1), 133–152. https://doi.org/10.1080/13854040701819050

Delis, D.C., Kramer, J.H., Kaplan, E., & Ober, B.A. (2000). *Manual for the California Verbal Learning Test, (CVLT-II).* The Psychological Corporation.

Detullio, D., Messer, S.C., Kennedy, T.D., & Millen, D.H. (2019). A meta-analysis of the Miller Forensic Assessment of Symptoms Test (M-FAST). *Psychological Assessment, 31*(11), 1319–1328. https://doi.org/10.1037/pas0000753

Duncan, A. (2005). The impact of cognitive and psychiatric impairment of psychotic disorders on the Test of Memory Malingering (TOMM). *Assessment, 12*(2), 123–129. https://doi.org/10.1177/1073191105275512

Etherton, J.L., Bianchini, K.J., Ciota, M.A., & Greve, K.W. (2005). Reliable digit span is unaffected by laboratory-induced pain: implications for clinical use. *Assessment, 12*(1), 101–106. https://doi.org/10.1177/1073191104270789

Faust, D., Hart, K.J., Guilmette, T.J., & Arkes, H.R. (1988). Neuropsychologists' capacity to detect adolescent malingerers. *Professional Psychology: Research and Practice, 19*(5), 508–515. https://doi.org/10.1037/0735-7028.19.5.508

Ferguson, R.J., Mittenberg, W., Barone, D.F., & Schneider, B. (1999). Postconcussion syndrome following sports-related head injury: Expectation as etiology. *Neuropsychology, 13*(4), 582–589. https://doi.org/10.1037/0894-4105.13.4.582

Fishbain, D.A., Rosomoff, H.L., Cutler, R.B. & Rosomoff, R.S. (1995). Secondary gain concept: a review of the scientific evidence. *The Clinical Journal of Pain, 11* (1), 6–21.

Gervais, R.O., Ben-Porath, Y.S., Wygant, D.B., & Green, P. (2007). Development and validation of a Response Bias Scale (RBS) for the MMPI-2. *Assessment, 14*(2), 196–208. https://doi.org/10.1177/1073191106295861

Gouvier, W.D., Cubic, B., Jones, G., Brantley, P., & Cutlip, Q. (1992). Postconcussion symptoms and daily stress in normal and head-injured college populations. *Archives of Clinical Neuropsychology, 7*(3), 193–211. https://doi.org/10.1016/0887-6177(92)90162-G

Green, P. (n.d.). *Green's Word Memory Test for Windows can now be administered in 17 languages.* Green's Word Memory Test. https://wordmemorytest.com/languages/

Green, P. (2003). *Manual for the Word Memory Test.* Green's Publishing Inc.

Green, P. (2004). *Medical Symptom Validity Test (MSVT) for Windows User's Manual.* Green's Publishing Inc.

Green, P. (2008). *Nonverbal Medical Symptom Validity Test (NV-MSVT for Windows User's Manual.* Green's Publishing Inc.

Green, P., & Flaro, L. (2003). Word Memory Test performance in children. *Child Neuropsychology, 9*(3), 189–207. https://doi.org/10.1076/chin.9.3.189.16460

Greiffenstein, M.F., Baker, W.J., & Gola, T. (1994). Validation of malingered amnesia measures with a large clinical sample. *Psychological Assessment, 6*(3), 218–224. https://doi.org/10.1037/1040-3590.6.3.218

Greve, K. (2004). Setting empirical cut-offs on psychometric indicators of negative response bias: A methodological commentary with recommendations. *Archives of Clinical Neuropsychology, 19*(4), 533–541. https://doi.org/10.1016/j.acn.2003.08.002

Greve, K.W., & Bianchini, K.J. (2004). Response to Butcher et al., The construct validity of the Lees-Haley Fake-Bad Scale. *Archives of Clinical Neuropsychology: The Official Journal of the National Academy of Neuropsychologists, 19*(3), 337–339; author reply 341–345. https://doi.org/10.1016/j.acn.2003.12.005

Greve, K.W., Bianchini, K.J., Love, J.M., Brennan, A., & Heinly, M.T. (2006). Sensitivity and specificity of MMPI-2 validity scales and indicators to malingered neurocognitive dysfunction in traumatic brain injury. *The Clinical Neuropsychologist, 20*(3), 491-512. https://doi.org/10.1080/13854040590967144

Greve, K.W., Binder, L.M., & Bianchini, K.J. (2009). Rates of below-chance performance in forced-choice symptom validity tests. *The Clinical Neuropsychologist, 23*(3), 534–544. https://doi.org/10.1080/13854040802232690

Greve, K.W., Heinly, M.T., Bianchini, K.J., & Love, J.M. (2009). Malingering detection with the Wisconsin Card Sorting Test in mild traumatic brain injury. *The Clinical Neuropsychologist, 23*(2), 343-362. https://doi.org/10.1080/13854040802054169

Greve, K.W., Love, J.M., Heinly, M.T., Doane, B.M., Uribe, E., Joffe, C.L., & Bianchini, K.J. (2005). Detection of feigned tactile sensory loss using a forced-choice test of tactile discrimination and other measures of tactile sensation. *Journal of Occupational and Environmental Medicine, 47*(7), 718–727. http://www.jstor.org/stable/44997448

Greve, K.W., Ord, J.S., Bianchini, K.J., & Curtis, K.L. (2009). Prevalence of malingering in patients with chronic pain referred for psychologic evaluation in a medico-legal context. *Archives of Physical Medicine and Rehabilitation, 90*(7), 1117–1126. https://doi.org/10.1016/j.apmr.2009.01.018

Gunstad, J., & Suhr, J.A. (2001). "Expectation as etiology" versus "the good old days": Postconcussion syndrome symptom reporting in athletes, headache sufferers, and depressed individuals. *Journal of the International Neuropsychological Society, 7*(3), 323–333. https://doi.org/10.1017/S1355617701733061

Heaton, R.K., Chelune, G.J., Talley, J.L., Kay, G.G., & Curtis, G. (1993). *Wisconsin Card Sorting Test (WCST) Manual.* Psychological Assessment Resources.

Heinly, M.T., Greve, K.W., Bianchini, K.J., Love, J.M., & Brennan, A. (2005). WAIS Digit Span-based indicators of malingered neurocognitive dysfunction: Classification accuracy in traumatic brain injury. *Assessment, 12*(4), 429–444. https://doi.org/10.1177/1073191105281099

Heinze, M.C., & Purisch, A.D. (2001). Beneath the mask: use of psychological tests to detect and subtype malingering in criminal defendants. *Journal of Forensic Psychology Practice, 1*(4), 23–52. https://doi.org/10.1300/J158v01n04_02

Henry, G.K., Heilbronner, R.L., Algina, J., & Kaya, Y. (2013). Derivation of the MMPI-2-RF Henry-Heilbronner Index-r (HHI-r) Scale. *The Clinical Neuropsychologist, 27*(3), 509–515. https://doi.org/10.1080/13854046.2012.739644

Institute of Medicine (U.S.). (2015). *Psychological Testing in the Service of Disability Determination.* The National Academies Press.

Iverson, G.L., & McCracken, L.M. (1997). "Postconcussive" symptoms in persons with chronic pain. *Brain Injury, 11*, 783–790. https://doi.org/10.1080/026990597122990

Jelicic, M., Merckelbach, H., Candel, I., & Geraerts, E. (2007). Detection of feigned cognitive dysfunction using special malinger tests: A simulation study in naïve and coached malingerers. *International Journal of Neuroscience, 117*(8), 1185–1192. https://doi.org/10.1080/00207450600934697

Kaplan, E., Goodglass, H., & Weintraub, S. (1983). *Boston naming test*. Lea & Febiger.

Kirkwood, M.W., Hargrave, D.D., & Kirk, J.W. (2011). The value of the WISC-IV Digit Span subtest in detecting noncredible performance during pediatric neuropsychological examinations. *Archives of Clinical Neuropsychology, 26*(5), 377–384. https://doi.org/10.1093/arclin/acr040

Kroenke, K., Spitzer, R.L., & Williams, J.B. (2002). The PHQ-15: validity of a new measure for evaluating the severity of somatic symptoms. *Psychosomatic Medicine, 64*(2), 258–266. https://doi.org/10.1097/00006842-200203000-00008

Kwan, O., Ferrari, R., & Friel, J. (2001). Tertiary gain and disability syndromes. *Medical Hypotheses, 57*(4), 459–464. https://doi.org/10.1054/mehy.2001.1360

Larrabee, G.J. (2003a). Detection of malingering using atypical performance patterns on standard neuropsychological tests. *The Clinical Neuropsychologist, 17*(3), 410–425. https://doi.org/10.1076/clin.17.3.410.18089

Larrabee, G.J. (2003b). Exaggerated pain report in litigants with malingered neurocognitive dysfunction. *The Clinical Neuropsychologist, 17*(3), 395–401. https://doi.org/10.1076/clin.17.3.395.18087

Larrabee, G.J. (2007). *Assessment of malingered neuropsychological deficits*. Oxford University Press. https://psycnet.apa.org/record/2007-10764-000

Larrabee, G.J. (2012a). Assessment of malingering. In G.J. Larrabee (Ed.), *Forensic Neuropsychology: A Scientific Approach* (2nd ed., pp. 116–159). Oxford University Press.

Larrabee, G.J. (2012b). Performance validity and symptom validity in neuropsychological assessment. *Journal of the International Neuropsychological Society, 18*(4), 625–630. https://doi.org/10.1017/S1355617712000240

Larrabee, G., Greiffenstein, M., Greve, K., & Bianchini, K. (2007). Refining diagnostic criteria for malingering. In G.J. Larrabee (Ed.), *Assessment of Malingered Neuropsychological Deficits* (pp. 334–371). Oxford University Press.

Lees-Haley, P.R., English, L.T., & Glenn, W.J. (1991). A Fake Bad Scale on the MMPI-2 for personal injury claimants. *Psychological Reports, 68*(1), 203–210. https://doi.org/10.2466/pr0.1991.68.1.203

Lezak, M.D. (Ed.). (2012). *Neuropsychological assessment* (5th ed.). Oxford University Press.

Lichtenstein, J.D., Erdodi, L.A., Rai, J.K., Mazur-Mosiewicz, A., & Flaro, L. (2018). Wisconsin Card Sorting Test embedded validity indicators developed for adults can be extended to children. *Child Neuropsychology, 24*(2), 247–260. https://doi.org/10.1080/09297049.2016.1259402

Main, C.J. (1983). The modified somatic perception questionnaire (MSPQ). *Journal of Psychosomatic Research, 27*(6), 503–514. https://doi.org/10.1016/0022-3999(83)90040-5

Marshall, P., & Happe, M. (2007). The performance of individuals with mental retardation on cognitive tests assessing effort and motivation. *The Clinical Neuropsychologist, 21*(5), 826–840. https://doi.org/10.1080/13854040600801001

Martin, P.K., Schroeder, R.W., & Odland, A.P. (2015). neuropsychologists' validity testing beliefs and practices: a survey of North American professionals. *The Clinical Neuropsychologist, 29*(6), 741–776. https://doi.org/10.1080/13854046.2015.1087597

Martin, P.K., Schroeder, R.W., Olsen, D.H., Maloy, H., Boettcher, A., Ernst, N., & Okut, H. (2020). A systematic review and meta-analysis of the Test of Memory Malingering in adults: Two decades of deception detection. *The Clinical Neuropsychologist, 34*(1), 88–119. https://doi.org/10.1080/13854046.2019.1637027

McCaul, C., Boone, K.B., Ermshar, A., Cottingham, M., Victor, T.L., Ziegler, E., Zeller, M.A., & Wright, M. (2018). Cross-validation of the Dot Counting Test in a large sample of credible and non-credible patients referred for neuropsychological testing. *The Clinical Neuropsychologist, 32*(6), 1054–1067. https://doi.org/10.1080/13854046.2018.1425481

Merten, T., Thies, E., Schneider, K., & Stevens, A. (2009). Symptom validity testing in claimants with alleged posttraumatic stress disorder: comparing the Morel Emotional Numbing Test, the Structured Inventory of Malingered Symptomatology, and the Word Memory Test. *Psychological Injury and Law, 2*(3–4), 284–293. https://doi.org/10.1007/s12207-009-9057-0

Meyers, J. (2002). A validity index for the MMPI-2. *Archives of Clinical Neuropsychology, 17*(2), 157–169. https://doi.org/10.1016/S0887-6177(00)00107-4

Meyers, J.E., & Volbrecht, M. (1998). Validation of reliable digits for detection of malingering. *Assessment, 5*(3), 303–307. https://doi.org/10.1177/107319119800500309

Meyers, J.E., Miller, R.M., Haws, N.A., Murphy-Tafiti, J.L., Curtis, T.D., Rupp, Z.W., Smart, T.A., & Thompson, L.M. (2014). An adaptation of the MMPI-2 Meyers Index for the MMPI-2-RF. *Applied Neuropsychology: Adult, 21*(2), 148–154. https://doi.org/10.1080/09084282.2013.780173

Miller, H.A. (2001). *Miller Forensic Assessment of Symptoms Test: Professional Manual.* Psychological Assessment Resources.

Miller, J.B., Millis, S.R., Rapport, L.J., Bashem, J.R., Hanks, R.A., & Axelrod, B.N. (2011). Detection of insufficient effort using the Advanced Clinical Solutions for the Wechsler Memory Scale, Fourth Edition. *The Clinical Neuropsychologist, 25*(1), 160–172. https://doi.org/10.1080/13854046.2010.533197

Millon, T., Grossman, S., & Millon, C. (2015). *MCMI-IV: Millon Clinical Multiaxial Inventory Manual.* NCS Pearson, Inc.

Mittenberg, W., & Strauman, S. (2000). Diagnosis of mild head injury and the postconcussion syndrome. *Journal of Head Trauma Rehabilitation, 15*(2), 783–791. https://doi.org/10.1097/00001199-200004000-00003

Mittenberg, W., DiGiulio, D.V., Perrin, S., & Bass, A.E. (1992). Symptoms following mild head injury: Expectation as aetiology. *Journal of Neurology, Neurosurgery & Psychiatry, 55*(3), 200–204. https://doi.org/10.1136/jnnp.55.3.200

Mittenberg, W., Patton, C., Canyock, E.M., & Condit, D.C. (2002). Base rates of malingering and symptom exaggeration. *Journal of Clinical and Experimental Neuropsychology, 24*(8), 1094–1102. https://doi.org/10.1076/jcen.24.8.1094.8379

Moore, B.A., & Donders, J. (2004). Predictors of invalid neuropsychological test performance after traumatic brain injury. *Brain Injury, 18*(10), 975–984. https://doi.org/10.1080/02699050410001672350

Morey, L. (2007). *The Personality Assessment Inventory Professional Manual* (2nd ed.). Psychological Assessment Resources.

Nelson, N.W., Hoelzle, J.B., Sweet, J.J., Arbisi, P.A., & Demakis, G.J. (2010). Updated meta-analysis of the MMPI-2 symptom validity scale (FBS): Verified utility in forensic practice. *The Clinical Neuropsychologist, 24*(4), 701–724. https://doi.org/10.1080/13854040903482863

Ozen, L.J., & Fernandes, M.A. (2010). Effects of "diagnosis threat" on cognitive and affective functioning long after mild head injury. *Journal of the International Neuropsychological Society, 17*(2), 219–229. https://doi.org/10.1017/S135561771000144X

Pertab, J.L., James, K.M., & Bigler, E.D. (2009). Limitations of mild traumatic brain injury meta-analyses. *Brain Injury, 23*(6), 498–508. https://doi.org/10.1080/02699050902927984

Pliskin, J.I., DeDios Stern, S., Resch, Z.J., Saladino, K.F., Ovsiew, G.P., Carter, D.A., & Soble, J.R. (2021). Comparing the psychometric properties of eight embedded performance validity tests in the Rey Auditory Verbal Learning Test, Wechsler Memory Scale Logical Memory, and Brief Visuospatial Memory Test – Revised Recognition Trials for detecting invalid neuropsychological test performance. *Assessment, 28*(8), 1871–1881. https://doi.org/10.1177/1073191120929093

Ponsford, J., Cameron, P., Fitzgerald, M., Grant, M., Mikocka-Walus, A., & Schönberger, M. (2012). Predictors of postconcussive symptoms 3 months after mild traumatic brain injury. *Neuropsychology, 26*, 304–313. https://doi.org/10.1037/a0027888

Rabin, L., Barr, W., & Burton, L. (2005). Assessment practices of clinical neuropsychologists in the United States and Canada: A survey of INS, NAN, and APA Division 40 members. *Archives of Clinical Neuropsychology, 20*(1), 33–65. https://doi.org/10.1016/j.acn.2004.02.005

Reese, C.S., Suhr, J.A., & Riddle, T.L. (2012). Exploration of malingering indices in the Wechsler Adult Intelligence Scale – Fourth Edition Digit Span Subtest. *Archives of Clinical Neuropsychology, 27*(2), 176–181. https://doi.org/10.1093/arclin/acr117

Rey, A. (1964). *L'Examen Clinique en Psychologie* [The clinical examination in psychology]. Presses Universitaires de France.

Reznek, L. (2005). The Rey 15-item memory test for malingering: A meta-analysis. *Brain Injury, 19*(7), 539–543. https://doi.org/10.1080/02699050400005242

Rhoads, T., Leib, S.I., Resch, Z.J., Basurto, K.S., Castillo, L.R., Jennette, K.J., & Soble, J.R. (2021). Relative rates of invalidity for the Test of Memory Malingering and the Dot Counting Test among Spanish-Speaking patients residing in the USA. *Psychological Injury and Law, 14*(4), 269–280. https://doi.org/10.1007/s12207-021-09423-z

Rhoads, T., Resch, Z.J., Ovsiew, G.P., White, D.J., Abramson, D.A., & Soble, J.R. (2021). Every second counts: A comparison of four dot counting test scoring procedures for detecting invalid neuropsychological test performance. *Psychological Assessment, 33*(2), 133–141. https://doi.org/10.1037/pas0000970

Rickards, T.A., Cranston, C.C., Touradji, P., & Bechtold, K.T. (2018). Embedded performance validity testing in neuropsychological assessment: Potential clinical tools. *Applied Neuropsychology: Adult, 25*(3), 219–230. https://doi.org/10.1080/23279095.2017.1278602

Rogers, R. (2001). *Handbook of diagnostic and structured interviewing*. Guilford Press.

Rogers, R., Babgy, R.M., & Dickens, S.E. (1992). *The Structured Interview of Reported Symptoms*. Psychological Assessment Resources.

Rogers, R., Harrell, E.H., & Liff, C.D. (1993). Feigning neuropsychological impairment: A critical review of methodological and clinical considerations. *Clinical Psychology Review, 13*(3), 255–274. https://doi.org/10.1016/0272-7358(93)90023-F

Rogers, R., Sewell, K., & Gillard, N. (2010). *Structured Inventory of Reported Symptoms Professional Manual* (2nd ed.). Psychological Assessment Resources.

Rohling, M.L., Binder, L.M., Demakis, G.J., Larrabee, G.J., Ploetz, D.M., & Langhinrichsen-Rohling, J. (2011). A meta-analysis of neuropsychological outcome after mild traumatic brain injury: Re-analyses and reconsiderations of Binder et al., Frencham et al., and Pertab et al. *The Clinical Neuropsychologist, 25*(4), 608–623. https://doi.org/10.1080/13854046.2011.565076

Rohling, M.L., Larrabee, G.J., & Millis, S.R. (2012). The "miserable minority" following mild traumatic brain injury: who are they and do meta-analyses hide them? *The Clinical Neuropsychologist, 26*(2), 197–213. https://doi.org/10.1080/13854046.2011.647085

Ruff, R.M., Iverson, G.L., Barth, J.T., Bush, S.S., Broshek, D.K., & the NAN Policy and Planning Committee. (2009). Recommendations for diagnosing a mild traumatic brain injury: A National Academy of Neuropsychology education paper. *Archives of Clinical Neuropsychology, 24*(1), 3–10. https://doi.org/10.1093/arclin/acp006

Schroeder, R.W., Twumasi-Ankrah, P., Baade, L.E., & Marshall, P.S. (2012). Reliable Digit Span: A systematic review and cross-validation study. *Assessment, 19*(1), 21–30. https://doi.org/10.1177/1073191111428764

Schwartz, E.S., Erdodi, L., Rodriguez, N., Ghosh, J.J., Curtain, J.R., Flashman, L.A., & Roth, R.M. (2016). CVLT-II Forced Choice Recognition Trial as an embedded validity indicator: A systematic review of the evidence. *Journal of the International Neuropsychological Society, 22*(8), 851–858. https://doi.org/10.1017/S1355617716000746

Sellbom, M., & Bagby, M. (2008). Response styles on multiscale inventories. In R. Rogers (Ed.), *Clinical assessment of malingering and deception* (2nd ed., pp. 182–206). Guilford Press.

Sherman, E., Tan, J., & Hrabok, M. (2023). *A Compendium of Neuropsychological Tests: Fundamentals of Neuropsychological Assessment and Test Reviews for Clinical Practice* (4th ed.). Oxford University Press.

Sherman, E.M. S., Slick, D.J., & Iverson, G.L. (2020). Multidimensional malingering criteria for neuropsychological assessment: A 20-year update of the malingered neuropsychological dysfunction criteria. *Archives of Clinical Neuropsychology, 35*(6), 735–764. https://doi.org/10.1093/arclin/acaa019

Shura, R.D., Brearly, T.W., Rowland, J.A., Martindale, S.L., Miskey, H.M., & Duff, K. (2018). RBANS validity indices: A systematic review and meta-analysis. *Neuropsychology Review, 28*(3), 269–284. https://doi.org/10.1007/s11065-018-9377-5

Silverberg, N.D., Iverson, G.L., Cogan, A., Dams-O-Connor, K., Delmonico, R., Graf, M.J. P., Iaccarino, M.A., Kajankova, M., Kamins, J., McCulloch, K.L., McKinney, G., Nagele, D., Panenka, W.J., Rabinowitz, A.R., Reed, N., Wethe, J.V., Whitehair, V., Anderson, V., Arciniegas, D.B., ... Zemek, R. (2023). The American Congress of Rehabilitation Medicine diagnostic criteria for mild traumatic brain injury. *Archives of Physical Medicine and Rehabilitation, 104*(8), 1343–1355. https://doi.org/10.1016/j.apmr.2023.03.036

Silverberg, N.D., Wertheimer, J.C., & Fichtenberg, N.L. (2007). An effort index for the Repeatable Battery for the Assessment of Neuropsychological Status (RBANS). *The Clinical Neuropsychologist, 21*(5), 841–854. https://doi.org/10.1080/13854040600850958

Slick, D.J., Hopp, G., Strauss, E., & Thompson, G.B. (1997). *Victoria Symptom Validity Test: Professional manual.* Psychological Assessment Resources.

Slick, D.J., Sherman, E.M. S., & Iverson, G.L. (1999). Diagnostic criteria for malingered neurocognitive dysfunction: Proposed standards for clinical practice and research. *The Clinical Neuropsychologist, 13*(4), 545–561. https://doi.org/10.1076/1385-4046(199911)13:04;1-Y;FT545

Smith, K., Boone, K., Victor, T., Miora, D., Cottingham, M., Ziegler, E., Zeller, M., & Wright, M. (2014). Comparison of credible patients of very low intelligence and non-credible patients on neurocognitive performance validity indicators. *The Clinical Neuropsychologist, 28*(6), 1048–1070. https://doi.org/10.1080/13854046.2014.931465

Social Security Administration. (2021). *Annual Statistical Report on the Social Security Disability Insurance Program* (Table 60). https://www.ssa.gov/policy/docs/statcomps/di_asr/2021/sect04.html#table60

Spielberg, S. (Director). (1982). *E. T. The extra-terrestrial.* [Video recording]. Universal Pictures.

Suhr, J. A., & Gunstad, J. (2002). "Diagnosis threat": The effect of negative expectations on cognitive performance in head injury. *Journal of Clinical and Experimental Neuropsychology, 24*(4), 448–457. https://doi.org/10.1076/jcen.24.4.448.1039

Suhr, J. A., & Gunstad, J. (2005). Further exploration of the effect of "diagnosis threat" on cognitive performance in individuals with mild head injury. *Journal of the International Neuropsychological Society, 11*(1), 23–29. https://doi.org/10.1017/S1355617705050010

Sullivan, M. J. L., Bishop, S. R., & Pivik, J. (1995). The Pain Catastrophizing Scale: Development and validation. *Psychological Assessment, 7*(4), 524–532. https://doi.org/10.1037/1040-3590.7.4.524

Teichner, G., & Wagner, M. T. (2004). The Test of Memory Malingering (TOMM): Normative data from cognitively intact, cognitively impaired, and elderly patients with dementia. *Archives of Clinical Neuropsychology, 19*(3), 455–464. https://doi.org/10.1016/S0887-6177(03)00078-7

Tombaugh, T. N. (1996). *Test of Memory Malingering (TOMM).* Multi-Health Systems, Inc.

Van Impelen, A., Merckelbach, H., Jelicic, M., & Merten, T. (2014). The Structured Inventory of Malingered Symptomatology (SIMS): A systematic review and meta-analysis. *The Clinical Neuropsychologist, 28*(8), 1336–1365. https://doi.org/10.1080/13854046.2014.984763

Vitacco, M. J., Rogers, R., Gabel, J., & Munizza, J. (2007). An evaluation of malingering screens with competency to stand trial patients: A known-groups comparison. *Law and Human Behavior, 31*(3), 249–260. https://doi.org/10.1007/s10979-006-9062-8

Widows, M. R., & Smith, G. P. (2005). *Structured Inventory of Malingered Symptomatology professional manual.* Psychological Assessment Resources.

World Health Organization. (2016). *International statistical classification of diseases and related health problems* (10th ed.). WHO. https://icd.who.int/browse10/2016/en

Wygant, D. B., Ben-Porath, Y. S., Arbisi, P. A., Berry, D. T., Freeman, D. B., & Heilbronner, R. L. (2009). Examination of the MMPI-2 restructured form (MMPI-2-RF) validity scales in civil forensic settings: Findings from simulation and known group samples. *Archives of Clinical Neuropsychology, 24*(7), 671–680. https://doi.org/10.1093/arclin/acp073

Wygant, D. B., Burchett, D., & Harp, J. P. (2019). Assessment of noncredible reporting and responding. In M. Sellbom & J. A. Suhr (Eds.), *The Cambridge Handbook of Clinical Assessment and Diagnosis* (1st ed., pp. 63–79). Cambridge University Press. https://doi.org/10.1017/9781108235433.006

Young, J. C., Roper, B. L., & Arentsen, T. J. (2016). Validity testing and neuropsychology practice in the VA healthcare system: Results from recent practitioner survey. *The Clinical Neuropsychologist, 30*(4), 497–514. https://doi.org/10.1080/13854046.2016.1159730

Appendix

Proposed Definition and Criteria for Possible, Probable, and Definite Malingering of Neurocognitive Dysfunction (MND)

Definition

Malingering of Neurocognitive Dysfunction (MND) is the volitional exaggeration or fabrication of cognitive dysfunction for the purpose of obtaining substantial material gain, or avoiding or escaping formal duty or responsibility. Substantial material gain includes money, goods, or services of nontrivial value (e.g., financial compensation for personal injury).

Formal duties are actions that people are legally obligated to perform (e.g., prison, military, or public service, or child support payments or other financial obligations). Formal responsibilities are those that involve accountability or liability in legal proceedings (e.g., competency to stand trial).

Diagnostic Categories for Malingering Neurocognitive Dysfunction (MND)

Definite MND

This is indicated by the presence of clear and compelling evidence of volitional exaggeration or fabrication of cognitive dysfunction and the absence of plausible alternative explanations. The specific diagnostic criteria necessary for Definite MND are listed below:

1. Presence of a substantial external incentive [Criterion A]
2. Definite negative response bias [Criterion B1]
3. Behaviors meeting necessary criteria from group B are not fully accounted for by Psychiatric, Neurological, or Developmental Factors [Criterion D]

Probable MND

This is indicated by the presence of evidence strongly suggesting volitional exaggeration or fabrication of cognitive dysfunction and the absence of plausible alternative explanations. The specific diagnostic criteria necessary for Probable MND are listed below:

1. Presence of a substantial external incentive [Criterion A]
2. Two or more types of evidence from neuropsychological testing, excluding definite negative response bias [two or more of Criteria B2–B6]

Or

One type of evidence from neuropsychological testing, excluding definite negative response bias, and one or more types of evidence from Self-Report [one of Criteria B2–B6 and one or more of Criteria C1–C5]

3. Behaviors meeting necessary criteria from groups B and C are not fully accounted for by Psychiatric, Neurological, or Developmental Factors [Criterion D]

Possible MND

This is indicated by the presence of evidence suggesting volitional exaggeration or fabrication of cognitive dysfunction and the absence of plausible alternative explanations. Alternatively, possible MND is indicated by the presence of criteria necessary for Definite or Probable MND except that other primary etiologies cannot be ruled out. The specific diagnostic criteria for Possible MND are listed below:

1. Presence of a substantial external incentive [Criterion A]
2. Evidence from Self-Report [one or more of Criteria C1–C5]
3. Behaviors meeting necessary criteria from group C are not fully accounted for by Psychiatric, Neurological, or Developmental Factors [Criterion D]

Or

Criteria for Definite or Probable MND are met except for Criterion D (i.e., primary psychiatric, neurological, or developmental etiologies cannot be ruled out). In such cases, the alternate etiologies that cannot be ruled out should be specified.

Explanation of Criteria

Criteria A: Presence of a Substantial External Incentive

At least one clearly identifiable and substantial external incentive for exaggeration or fabrication of symptoms (see definition) is present at the time of examination (e.g., personal injury settlement, disability pension, evasion of criminal prosecution, or release from military service).

Criteria B: Evidence From Neuropsychological Testing

Evidence of exaggeration or fabrication of cognitive dysfunction on neuropsychological tests, as demonstrated by at least one of the following.

1. *Definite negative response bias.* Below chance performance ($p<.05$) on one or more forced-choice measures of cognitive function.
2. *Probable response bias.* Performance on one or more *well-validated* psychometric tests or indices designed to measure exaggeration or fabrication of cognitive deficits is consistent with feigning.
3. *Discrepancy between test data and known patterns of brain functioning.* A pattern of neuropsychological test performance that is markedly discrepant from currently accepted models of normal and abnormal central nervous system (CNS) function. The discrepancy must be consistent with an attempt to exaggerate or fabricate neuropsychological dysfunction (e.g., a patient performs in the severely impaired range on verbal attention measures but in the average range on memory testing; a patient misses items on recognition t esting that were consistently provided on previous free recall trials, or misses many easy items when significantly harder items from the same test are passed).
4. *Discrepancy between test data and observed behavior.* Performance on two or more neuropsychological tests within a domain are discrepant with observed level of cognitive function in a way that suggests exaggeration or fabrication of dysfunction (e.g., a well-educated patient who presents with no significant visual-perceptual deficits or language disturbance in conversational speech performs in the severely impaired range on verbal fluency and confrontation naming tests).
5. *Discrepancy between test data and reliable collateral reports.* Performance on two or more neuropsychological tests within a domain are discrepant with day-to-day level of cognitive function described by at least one reliable collateral informant in a way that suggests exaggeration or fabrication of dysfunction (e.g., a patient handles all family finances but is unable to perform simple math problems in testing).

6. *Discrepancy between test data and documented background history.* Improbably poor performance on two or more standardized tests of cognitive function within a specific domain (e.g., memory) that is inconsistent with documented neurological or psychiatric history (e.g., a patient with no documented LOC or PTA, multiple negative neurological investigations, and no other history of CNS trauma or disease consistently obtains verbal memory scores in the severely impaired range after a motor vehicle accident).

Criteria C: Evidence From Self-Report

The following behaviors are indicators of possible malingering of cognitive deficits, but their presence is not sufficient for the diagnosis. However, presence of one or more of these criteria provides additional evidence in support of a diagnosis of malingering. These criteria involve significant inconsistencies or discrepancies in the patient's self-reported symptoms that suggest a deliberate attempt to exaggerate or fabricate cognitive deficits.

1. *Self-reported history is discrepant with documented history.* Reported history is markedly discrepant with documented medical or psychosocial history and suggests attempts to exaggerate injury severity or deny premorbid neuropsychological dysfunction (e.g., exaggerated severity of physical injury or length of LOC/PTA; exaggerated premorbid educational or occupational achievement; denial of previous head injury or previous psychiatric history).
2. *Self-reported symptoms are discrepant with known patterns of brain functioning.* Reported or endorsed symptoms are improbable in number, pattern, or severity; or markedly inconsistent with expectations for the type or severity of documented injury or pathology (e.g., claims of extended retrograde amnesia without loss of memory for the accident, or claims of loss of autobiographical information after mild head trauma without LOC).
3. *Self-reported symptoms are discrepant with behavioral observations.* Reported symptoms are markedly inconsistent with observed behavior (e.g., a patient complains of severe episodic memory deficits yet has little difficulty remembering names, events, or appointments; a patient complains of severe cognitive deficits yet has little difficulty driving independently and arrives on time for an appointment in an unfamiliar area; a patient complains of severely slowed mentation and concentration problems yet easily follows complex conversation).
4. *Self-reported symptoms are discrepant with information obtained from collateral informants.* Reported symptoms, history, or observed behavior is in-

consistent with information obtained from other informants judged to be adequately reliable. The discrepancy must be consistent with an attempt to exaggerate injury severity or deny premorbid neuropsychological dysfunction (e.g., a patient reports severe memory impairment and/or behaves as if severely memory-impaired, but their spouse reports that the patient has minimal memory dysfunction at home).

5. *Evidence of exaggerated or fabricated psychological dysfunction.* Self-reported symptoms of psychological dysfunction are substantially contradicted by behavioral observation and/or reliable collateral information. *Well-validated* validity scales or indices on self-report measures of psychological adjustment (e.g., MMPI-2) are strongly suggestive of exaggerated or fabricated distress or dysfunction.

Criteria D: Behaviors Meeting Necessary Criteria From Groups B or C Are Not Fully Accounted for by Psychiatric, Neurological, or Developmental Factors

Behaviors meeting necessary criteria from groups B and C are the product of an informed, rational, and volitional effort aimed at least in part towards acquiring or achieving external incentives as defined in Criteria A. As such, behaviors meeting criterion from groups B or C cannot be fully accounted for by psychiatric, developmental, or neurological disorders that result in significantly diminished capacity to appreciate laws or mores against malingering, or inability to conform behavior to such standards (e.g., psychological need to "play the sick role", or in response to command hallucinations).

Peer Commentaries

This handbook provides a comprehensive yet concise overview of validity assessment within psychological and neuropsychological evaluations. By detailing the critical role of symptom and performance validity testing, the text offers accessible guidance on integrating these measures into routine clinical practice. It serves as an excellent resource for experienced practitioners as well as clinicians new to neuropsychological evaluations seeking to strengthen the rigor of their validity assessment protocols.

Bradley N. Axelrod, PhD, ABN, John D. Dingell Department of Veterans Affairs Medical Center, Detroit, MI

This well written book exploring the use of performance and symptom validity measures commonly used in the field of neuropsychology could easily become an indispensable desk reference for practitioners. It provides clinicians with a resource for understanding and applying methods to evaluate the validity of assessment data – an essential component of accurate interpretation. I can recommend this to any reader seeking a concise, well-articulated guide to validity assessment.

John Meyers, PsyD, ABN, Meyers Neuropsychological Services, Clermont, FL